"Therefore be on the alert, remembering that day and night for a period of

Three Years I did not cease to admonish each one with tears." Acts 20:31

(Apostle Paul to the elders at Ephesus)

Printed by CreateSpace, An Amazon.com Company

Available on Amazon.com and other online stores

Author's Note: Most of the stories in this book are actual, true life events. A few of the stories are allegorical, although they may be based on real events. Many names of persons described have been changed to protect their privacy.

TABLE OF CONTENTS

CONVERSION > SPIRITUAL GROWTH > TRAINING>RELEASE INTO MINISTRY

MODELING   TARGETED TEACHING   PERSONAL TRAINING   RELEASE

TRANSFORMING   CALL

PROLOGUE

I once heard about a man named Dee that had been in ministry for a long time. Dee's reputation preceded him. Dee ran an outreach to children. He had led a children's ministry club for many years. He was known in ministry circles citywide as a model for dynamic leadership. I was eager to meet Dee and to learn from him.

Dee was a large, muscular and handsome man. But Dee wasn't just physically appealing, he was very charismatic. Dee had "presence." When you met Dee, you immediately liked him. When he spoke, he commanded your attention. He had a deep, booming voice. Dee was entertaining...and funny! He told stories and jokes. Like many others, I was enthralled.

Dee proceeded to describe his ministry. Over the years, thousands of children had come to his after school Bible clubs. The children had received care, and had heard Dee share many times. Dee was animated as he described the size and scope of his work. I could see why he was so popular.

Then I asked, "How are the older children doing now?"

Dee paused. "What do you mean?"

"The children that were in the club ten years ago," I responded. "How are they doing now?"

Dee's brow furrowed. "I don't know."

"Where are they now?"

"I don't know. They moved on. They got too old to come to the club."

"Do you stay in contact with them?"

"Well, I would like to, of course, but I just don't have time. I'm so busy with the children who are in my clubs now. There are so many, I can barely turn around."

I left that meeting thankful for Dee and his work. His club meetings were big events. But something bothered me. Dee had contact with so many, yet he didn't know whether his work had long term influence on them or not. Was his ministry really effective? I didn't know.

I thought to myself, "I want permanence. But how can a person function in a way that has lasting impact?"

LESSON 1 - WHAT WERE JESUS' INSTRUCTIONS?

It was the first day of soccer practice. I coached a high school soccer team. On the first day of practice, I watched the freshmen carefully. They were the new players. I knew what to expect from the returning upperclassmen. I had seen them play, and I had a pretty good idea of what they could do. So I tended to focus on the freshmen. I wanted to see what they could do, even if what they demonstrated at that stage was often more potential than talent.

And I focused on the freshmen for another reason. Just as I had an idea of what to expect from the upperclassmen, the upperclassmen knew what to expect from soccer practice and from me. They had already participated in scores of practices. But the freshmen - they did not know what to expect at soccer practice. Most of the freshmen had played junior high soccer, and a few had just played recreation league. At those levels, guys play for fun. A player gets playing time just by showing up.

But the varsity level was different. Playing time was earned. Making the team was earned. Some of these freshmen would be cut before the season began. I focused on the freshmen to see how they responded. Players at the varsity level were bigger, faster, and rougher than most of the freshmen had ever seen. And the practices - the practices were tougher than they had ever experienced.

Freshmen were accustomed to playing soccer at soccer practices. But my early season practices focused on conditioning and fundamentals. My teams might not even play a scrimmage game for two weeks. And the first practice - it was all about conditioning. We did drills - running, dribbling, jumping, cutting, sprinting and then more running - all in the withering heat and humidity of early August.

Thirty minutes into the first practice, the team was running "suicides" - sprints of varying distances...up and back... up and back... up and back - over and over and over again. I watched the red faced players closely - their cheeks huffing, their sides heaving, and sweat pouring down their faces. At the end of each suicide, the freshmen were bent over, holding onto their shorts for support, panting for breath.

One of the freshmen looked up at me. In between his gasps for air, he asked,

"Are...are we done...are we done yet?" An upperclassman near him snorted.

"Are we done yet?" Are we done yet! I thought about what I knew, and what that freshman did not know. I thought about the remainder of the first practice. More suicides. Then weaving and leaping drills. Then push ups, sit-ups and thrusts. Then sprints. And at the end, long distance running. Lap after lap - running for miles.

"Are we done yet?" I thought of the rest of the season. More practices and more conditioning - never less; always more. Then scrimmages, and finally games. The first game - where no matter how hard we conditioned in our practices, my team invariably tired before the game ended. The only way to get in real "game condition" was to play the games themselves.

"Are we done yet?" I thought of the fierce competition - the ups and downs of a season. Players got hurt, but played through the pain. Injuries occurred. There would be team trips in the van, and arguments among teammates. Team meals after games and the camaraderie of shared exhaustion. Referees made questionable calls. Fans cheered, yelled and screamed. We would experience close wins and elation, and we would experience losses and disappointments.

"Are we done yet?" I looked back at the player and slowly shook my head. I blew my whistle. "Line up to run again!"

ARE WE DONE YET?

"Are we done yet?" Jesus' disciples had the same question. They had followed Jesus for three years. The ministry had been very difficult. Jesus' response to one "would be" follower was – "The foxes have holes and the birds of the air have nests, but the Son of Man has nowhere to lay his head." Lk. 9:58. The ministry had not yielded much material prosperity or comfort. When tax time came, Peter was required to extract the money miraculously from a fish to make the payment. Mt. 17:27. The disciples had been through a lot.

"Are we done yet?" But the disciples had heard about the "kingdom." They expected Jesus to establish His Kingdom at any time. That expectation grew as Jesus approached Jerusalem. Some of the disciples were jockeying for positions within Jesus' administration. Mt.

20:21. Even at the end of Jesus' earthly ministry, immediately before Jesus ascended back to His Father, the disciples asked Him, "Is it at this time that You are restoring the kingdom to Israel?" Acts 1:6.

"Are we done yet?" The disciples had that expectation as Jesus neared Jerusalem. They "supposed that the Kingdom of God was going to appear immediately." Lk. 19:11. The disciples were a tired group, but they harbored high hopes that the hard times were coming to an end.

"Are we done yet?" In response to this question, Jesus told His disciples a parable. "He went on to tell a parable, because He was near Jerusalem, and they supposed that the Kingdom of God was going to appear immediately." Lk. 19:11.

PARABLES

Parables are important. Every time Jesus tells a parable, followers of Jesus should pay special attention. In Matthew 13, Jesus' disciples asked Him why he spoke in parables. Jesus' response makes it clear that parables are told specifically to, and for the benefit of, His followers. His parables contain "mysteries of the Kingdom of heaven" intended only for His disciples. Mt. 13:11ff. Furthermore, His parables contain "things hidden since the foundation of the world." Mt. 13:35.

Things hidden since the foundation of the world! When I study a parable, I don't just read it a time or two. I read it again and again - day after day. I mull over it. I pray about it. I meditate on it. I sift it. I ask the Holy Spirit to reveal to me the "mysteries of the Kingdom of heaven" contained in it. Parables are important. We should pay attention.

JESUS' RESPONSE TO "ARE WE DONE YET?"

"Are we done yet?" In response to the disciples' expectation that the hard work would soon end and that kingdom glory was around the corner, Jesus told His disciples the parable of the minas. Lk. 19:8-27. In the parable, a nobleman goes far away to receive a kingdom. Before he departs, he gives ten of his servants each a "mina," and instructs them to "do business" with it. When the nobleman returns as a king, he requires an accounting by each servant of what he did with the mina entrusted to him.

What is Jesus communicating to His disciples with this parable? First, Jesus corrects the disciples' notion that their work was ending soon.

Through this parable, Jesus is saying "Your work is not finished. I am not receiving the Kingdom now. I (the nobleman) am going away to a place where I will receive the Kingdom. In my absence, there is work for you to do. I am giving you each a 'mina' - something of great worth. You transact business with it until I return. I expect an increase in minas. Your work is not finished. In fact, your work is only beginning!"

REPRODUCTION

But Jesus does more than address the disciples' mistaken idea about their work. In the same parable, Jesus tells the disciples exactly what type of work Jesus expects them to do.

In the parable of the minas, when the nobleman returns, he calls his servants to him to give an account. Two of the servants had been hard at work with their minas. They reported "Master, your mina has made ten minas more" (Lk. 19:16), and "Your mina, Master, has made five minas more" (Lk. 19:18). These obedient servants were rewarded generously for their service.

What Jesus is illustrating in this parable is the PRINCIPLE OF REPRODUCTION. It is His desire that his disciples labor in the currency of the Kingdom and that they reproduce it.

PRINCIPLE: The business of the Kingdom of God is REPRODUCTION.

"BE FRUITFUL AND MULTIPLY..."

My wife and I were at a small group meeting from our church. My wife was young - in her early 20's. She had bright prospects in front of her - the possibilities of career and marriage. Her future was wide open.

During prayer time in the meeting, another group member opened her eyes and looked directly at my wife. Speaking in a tone as if she had a "word from the Lord," the other member said, "You will have children."

What surprised me was not the word itself. It wasn't really a daring word. To tell a young and pretty woman that she would have children was not exactly "going out on a limb."

What surprised me was my wife's reaction. My wife paused for a minute to let the statement sink in. Then she burst into tears. The tears were not tears of grief. It was as if the word had expressed her whole heart. Her instincts, her desires, her longings - they were captured by those four words, "You will have children."

In so many areas, God has created natural instincts in us that mirror spiritual principles. Marriage, for example, reflects the intimacy of Christ and the church. The physical aspects of our lives help us understand our spiritual DNA.

Have you ever wondered why God placed in our bodies such a strong desire to reproduce physically? If we have Holy Spirit DNA, we have the same intense desire to reproduce spiritually. In the same way that men and women have a natural drive to produce offspring, the truly spiritual person has a burning drive to reproduce spiritually.

The instruction to reproduce is reiterated throughout scripture. "Be fruitful and multiply..." That instruction is repeated to Adam (Gen. 1:28); to Noah (Gen. 9:1); and to Jacob (Gen. 35:11). God intends that His world be well populated with living bodies. God likewise intends that His Kingdom be well populated with living souls.

"Be fruitful and multiply..." Jesus gives the same charge to His disciples - then and now. How amazing that reproduction is the instruction that Jesus left!

WHAT DO WE REPRODUCE?

What is a mina? A mina was literally a measurement of weight. In Jesus' time, a mina of gold or silver was a large sum of money.

In the parable, the nobleman gives a mina to each servant as capital. He instructs them to "do business with it." Is there capital in the Kingdom of God? What is the currency that Jesus gives to do the business of the Kingdom of God?

The context and content of the parable give us some clues:

1. The introduction of the parable begins "While they were listening to these things, [Jesus] went on to tell a parable..." Lk. 19:11. Listening to what things? Immediately before this parable, Jesus visited Zaccheus and ultimately proclaimed "Today salvation has come to this house... For the Son of Man came to seek and to save that which was lost." Lk. 19:9-10. The parable is told in the context of the salvation of the lost.

2. Use of the mina involves sowing and reaping. "You take up what you did not lay down, and reap what you did not sow." Lk. 19:21-22. With what do Jesus' servants sow and reap?

I believe that the mina represents the *gospel* - the word of the Kingdom. The Holy Spirit illuminates the gospel to each believer, resulting in eternal salvation. The gospel is retained permanently within each believer, but it is not confined there. The gospel is meant to be shared. The gospel should be "put into play" - reproduced within the hearts of its hearers. The gospel is "the word implanted which is able to save your souls." Jm. 1:21.

The currency of the Kingdom is the gospel. In his commentary on this passage, Matthew Henry says "They that trade diligently and faithfully in the service of Christ shall be gainers...The conversion of souls is the winning of them; every true convert is clear gain to Jesus Christ."

PRINCIPLE: Jesus has given us the gospel to put into play.

There was a fair amount of excitement among the members of Faith Fellowship. The little church needed a boost. A couple of years before, the congregation had been much larger. A split in the church had occurred, though, and many members departed. A few months after the split, the young pastor decided to move to Oklahoma in order to receive more training. The few remaining members of the church suffered some discouragement.

Lately, though, the church had reason for hope. The church met in a small storefront in Elmore, Alabama. The church held a revival week. A local family that resided a few doors down from the church came to the revival. The parents in the family accepted

the Lord and the family joined Faith Fellowship as members. This good news boosted the morale of the church.

At the Wednesday night prayer meeting a couple of weeks later, the new family was in attendance. Before preaching, however, a couple of the family members slipped out of the service. Then, shortly before eight o'clock, the rest of the family left out the back door. They did not return. There was some concern about the family.

Elder Tom decided he better go check and make sure that the family was okay. When Elder Tom returned a little while later, the members stopped the service to get a report. Had something gone wrong?

"Well," Elder Tom started, "as I came to the front door, I could see through the living room window. The whole family was sitting there watching television! I knocked on the front door, and the father came to the door and opened it.

"'Is everything okay?' I asked. 'You left in kind of a hurry.'

"He looked kind of embarrassed, then said, 'Our favorite television show comes on at eight o'clock on Wednesday nights.'

"'Um, shouldn't you be in church on Wednesday nights?'

"He stared at me strangely, and then asked, 'Elder Tom, we came to the church revival meeting, didn't we?'

"'Yes, you did.'

"'And we joined the church and became members, didn't we?'

"'Yes.'

"'Well, Elder Tom, if we came and we joined the church, what else do you want from us?'

At that point, Elder Tom stopped. His face showed a little consternation, "What did you say, Elder Tom?" another church member inquired.

"At that point, I really didn't know what to say. I just said, 'You should be in church instead of watching television.' I then said 'Good bye,' and left."

This story is a true one. The father of the family thought that church membership fulfilled his religious duty. Elder Tom expected not only church membership, but church participation.

9

What did Jesus expect of His disciples?

"Go therefore and make disciples of all nations..." Mt. 28:19-20. This statement summarizes Jesus' final instruction to His disciples at the end of each gospel (Mk. 16:15; Lk. 24:49; Jn. 20:21), and at the beginning of the Book of Acts (Acts 1:8). It is spiritual reproduction. Think of what Jesus did not say:

1. Jesus didn't say... "Put your resources in a building program and build large buildings as monuments to me." Do such buildings glorify God alone, or do they glorify others as well?

2. Jesus didn't say... "Take the good news that I have given you. Hunker down and just hang on until I get back." Sometimes we feel that hunkering is all we can do, but God has proactive plans.

3. Jesus didn't say..."Focus on your own spirituality. Engage in massive individual growth."

4. Jesus didn't say... "Enroll members to your church so that you have a huge organization."

These activities can be good goals, IF they lead to reproduction of permanent disciples. Growing church membership and increasing church attendance can be positive indicators. But if they do not result in obedient and active followers of Jesus, then they may actually be futile, or even detrimental, activities.

PRINCIPLE: Jesus' instruction to His followers was to make disciples of all nations.

WHAT ABOUT THE ALTERNATIVE?

There is another poignant principle depicted by Jesus in the parable of the minas. It is a principle illustrated by the slave who did not "get busy" with his mina. Instead, he disobeyed and hid his mina. Lk. 19:20.

It is the same principle experienced by the rich young ruler. He was called by Jesus to be

Jesus' disciple, but he was not willing to give up his riches to do the Master's bidding. Scripture says "He went away grieved." Mk. 10:22. His disobedience led to REGRET.

It is the principle experienced by the "rich fool." He understood about production and about being busy. In his business, he planted crops and produced fruit. Sowing and reaping was something he did all the time. But he was busy for his own benefit and not for the Lord. "Thou fool! This very night your soul is required of you..." Lk.12:20. His disobedience led to eternal death.

In the parable of the minas, the foolish slave possessed the gift from the Lord. He named the name of his Lord; he was one of His slaves. He may have been an excellent slave in all but one regard. But that slave showed he was not submitted to the will and Lordship of his Master, because he did not obey the command to do business with the gift which he received. He did not reproduce it.

That slave experienced a harsh judgement. "By your own words I will judge you, you worthless slave." Lk. 19:22. His own Master determined him "worthless," and the very gift he received was taken from him. He experienced the harsh consequence of disobedience.

> PRINCIPLE: Disobedience leads to regret.

MEDITATION: Hear these words of Jesus: "Blessed is the man whom the Master finds doing His will when He comes." Lk. 12:43.

1. This verse is told in the context of a steward waiting for his Master to return. Lk. 12:36-42. What is Jesus' expectation of His followers?

2. What stewardship has Jesus entrusted to you as His follower?

3. If Jesus returned now, what accounting would you give to Him?

REVIEW:

1. Jesus let His disciples know that their work was just beginning.

2. The business of the Kingdom of God is reproduction.

3. Jesus has given us the gospel to put into play.

4. Jesus' final instruction was to make disciples of all nations.

5. All followers of Jesus are called to make disciples.

6. Disobedience leads to regret.

LESSON 2 - A SCARY MOMENT

My father was a college professor. His teaching methods were unusual. When my older sister approached driving age, my family piled into our big Ford Econoline van and went to an open paved area where my father planned to teach my sister how to drive. My dad found some empty milk cartons, laid them on the pavement van-width apart, and told my sister to drive through them while he stood outside the van and watched.

Tightly clenching the steering wheel with one hand while wrestling with the "three on the tree" gearshift with the other, my sister tried to navigate the makeshift obstacle course. She ran over a milk jug on the right. "You just killed the baby on the right!" my father yelled. "Back up and try again!"

As we younger children watched in fascination, my sister regrouped for another run. She overcorrected. "You killed the baby on the left! Watch where you are going!" Daddy shouted.

My sister was now sweating. She was clearly shaken as she braced for a third try. She veered right, and then jerked the steering wheel left. "Now you killed two babies - one on the right and one on the left!" The frustration in my father's voice was evident. Over the course of the lesson, his exasperation increased as my sister's angst likewise grew. More babies died. I don't think anyone was particularly pleased by the driving lesson that day.

When my turn for a driving lesson came, I didn't even get the benefit of a running start. My father took me out in an old VW bug with a straight drive transmission. He stopped uphill on an incline in the mountains of western North Carolina, put the car in neutral, pulled on the hand brake, and told me to switch seats. I got in the driver's seat and looked down at the array of pedals - the accelerator, the brake pedal and the clutch.

Driving a straight drive is challenging enough. In order to stop the car, you push in the clutch with your left foot, and depress the brake pedal with your right foot. To start forward again, you take your right foot off the brake and press the accelerator with it, while simultaneously letting off the clutch with your left foot so that you don't roll backwards. It takes quickness and skill, especially if you are on a hill. I had never driven a straight drive vehicle.

On my first attempt, I wasn't quick enough. As I slowly let off the brake to push the accelerator, the car just started rolling backwards. My father reached over and pulled up the handle of the emergency brake to stop the car. "You have to be quick, son," he said. "Don't dilly-dally when you are going up a hill."

I took deep breath and tried again, but I didn't give it enough gas. The car stalled, and I scrambled to stop the car with the brakes. "You didn't press the accelerator hard enough, son! You have to give it a lot of gas to get up the hill," my father said. His voice had a tinge of irritation.

I restarted the car. I revved the motor good this time - so much so that the car jerked when I let out the clutch, and the engine died again. "Too much gas!" my father shouted. "Give it the right amount of gas with your right foot while you feel the clutch with your left foot!"

I was getting flustered. I had no idea what "feeling the clutch" meant. I started the car and tried to get it to go, but I failed again...and again...and again. Daddy did everything he could. He taught, lectured, cajoled and yelled. But as my failures mounted, my father's frustration increased. And as his frustration increased, my inability to start that car up that hill increased as well.

That "lesson" seemed to last a painful eternity. Despite dozens of tries, I never got the car going. Finally, with resignation in his voice, my father said, "Oh well, let's just go home."

Deflated, I got out of the driver's seat and we switched back. "See, you do it like this!" my father said. And he started the car up the hill emphatically. I slumped in my seat. I felt like a complete failure.

The next morning, I got ready for school. As I was packing my books, my father came into the room. "Here, son," he said, "drive your brothers to school." Then he threw me the keys to the VW bug. I was stunned. Not only was my father telling me, the Failure, to drive that same car. He was trusting me to give his other sons a ride in it as well! I was astounded! As I walked out the door, I realized that I was very scared.

Failure followed by responsibility. It is an amazing feeling of awe and fear. I was a complete failure at driving. But to be handed the keys to the car on the heels of that failure was stunning!

Failure followed by responsibility. It is something that happened in the Bible. At the crucial moment - the moment of the cross – Jesus' disciples deserted him. They completely failed him. Especially Peter who, just a few hours earlier, had boldly proclaimed that he would die for Jesus. Jn. 13:37. Yet there Peter stood - surrounded in the courtyard by Jesus' accusers, denying his relationship with Jesus - repeatedly. Then Peter beheld Jesus' gaze. Lk. 22:61. Overwhelmed by his failure, Peter fled and wept bitterly. Lk. 22:62.

Despite their failures, the disciples later stood on a mountain together with Jesus. He gave them final instructions - to witness to the whole earth and to make disciples of all nations. Then He departed. Now it was all in their hands - the Kingdom of God, the church, the bride. It was up to them! They now had the full responsibility!

As afraid as I felt when my father threw me the keys, Jesus' apostles must have felt much greater apprehension as they stood on that mountaintop. How could Jesus expect those failures to fulfill His instructions?

For three years, Jesus was the focal point of the ministry. He was the Source of power and miracles. He was the Teacher - prepared with every precise and discerning Word - able to foil the shrewdest intellectual devices contrived by human genius. He was the disciples' Rock of protection in the midst of every storm. Jesus was the Ministry.

If the disciples made a mess, Jesus cleaned it up. If they lost direction, Jesus refocused them. If they erred, Jesus corrected them. Jesus provided compassion, love and forgiveness. He took care of them.

But now, Jesus was gone. The whole future of the Church, Jesus' bride, rested with them. The fulfillment of God's plans on earth lay in their hands. The whole future of the Kingdom depended on the lives of a few men. How could Jesus leave them with such a burden at this critical juncture in history?

The answer is simple. Jesus had personally discipled them! Jesus had shown them, taught them and trained them to do the work of the Kingdom! Jesus had poured Himself into those twelve men. Then, on that mountaintop, He released them.

And in making those disciples, Jesus left a model for all of His followers to use. We can learn from Jesus and study how He made disciples. We can learn the lessons of Jesus like His disciples did.

PRINCIPLE: Jesus could leave His ministry to His disciples because He had discipled them.

JESUS' MODEL

Jesus chose twelve disciples. Jesus focused on just a few. Jesus ministered to many people, and He had other followers. But Jesus chose twelve disciples. It was those twelve that the Father gave Him, and it was those twelve that He guarded. "While I was with them, I was keeping them in Thy Name which Thou hast given Me; and I guarded them, and not one of them perished but the son of perdition, that the Scripture might be fulfilled." Jn. 17:12. Jesus knew those twelve disciples assured the future of the Kingdom IF they would learn from Him and obey Him.

When many people think of discipleship, they think of conversion.

For many years, I have participated in a sports outreach to young men. Through soccer, we cultivated relationships with hundreds of soccer players - most of who were of diverse nationality and from different religious backgrounds. Because of these relationships, we had many opportunities to share about life and about our faith. One event that I loved was an annual weekend soccer camp that we sponsored for the guys. The soccer camp provided a forum to share testimony publicly with the participants. Even more meaningful to me, the camp was an occasion to sit down with one or two young men at a time and to hear their hearts. I could then share from my own heart.

My close friend, Sam, was passionate for the gospel. Sam loved to hear news of our sports outreach. He prayed fervently for these camps and for the young men attending them.

After one camp, Sam and I had lunch. He was eager to hear a report of the weekend. The first question out of his mouth as we sat down was "Well, did you get any

conversions?"

I squirmed a little bit at his "cut to the chase" question. "No," I said, "we did not have any conversions." Sam looked disappointed.

"But," I continued, "we had forty guys come to the camp. The gospel was proclaimed. The Word was shared. Seeds were planted in hearts. Young men from Christian homes were affirmed in their faith. But maybe most importantly, we built relationships with non-Christians through which we can share and continue to influence lives."

I paused and looked at Sam. "Sam, I want permanence. Conversions are important and you know that we have had conversions and baptisms. Those occasions are joyful. But the final goal is to make disciples – to make reproducing disciples. Conversion is the starting point of that goal. I am trying to build into guys' lives - to build lasting relationships and lasting discipleship that, with God's help, will endure a lifetime."

Sam had a thoughtful look on his face. He slowly nodded his head. "Tell me more about the camp," he said.

Conversion is vital. But it is only the beginning of discipleship. Just as vital is effective ministry after conversion. Making a disciple is hard relational work. It involves a progression in the life of the disciple:

CONVERSION > SPIRITUAL GROWTH > TRAINING   > RELEASE INTO MINISTRY

A. CONVERSION - Conversion is the pure work of the Holy Spirit bringing a soul to salvation, usually by the sharing of the Gospel. Through repentance and baptism, the new disciple experiences a life change - moving out of the kingdom of darkness into the Kingdom of light; from an existence driven by the flesh to a life led by God's Spirit.

B. SPIRITUAL GROWTH - Spiritual growth is the process of spiritual maturation within the believer. Growth includes the following areas:

1. Christian Beliefs - Knowing and understanding what a Christian believes.

2. Personal Character - Growth in personal character leading to Christlikeness. The

disciple cultivates the traits of Christ within himself, and exhibits them on a consistent basis.

3. Christian Disciplines - Change of personal habits to include regular prayer, worship, Bible study, meditation and fellowship. These changes result in a Christian lifestyle.

4. Christian Witness - This witness arises from our being (who Christ is within us), and our doing (the Holy Spirit acting through us).

C. TRAINING - Training includes instructing and equipping the disciple for every good work. Personal training assists the disciple in identifying his calling(s), and learning how to function in a way that fulfills that ministry.

D. RELEASE INTO MINISTRY - At this point, the disciple is a mature Christian, and is able to operate independently in his ministry. Mindful that a believer is always connected to and dependent on other believers, the disciple is commissioned and then released to make disciples on his own.

Jesus followed this progression with His disciples. He kept them close to His side, nurturing, teaching and training them. His relationship with His disciples was deep and lasting. This model of Jesus flowed from His plan for His disciples.

WHAT WAS JESUS' PLAN FOR HIS DISCIPLES?

During a part of my life, the following was my regular ministry schedule:

1. Attend church with my family on Sunday mornings.

2. Coach soccer weekly with 10-30 refugee and inner city youth on Sunday afternoons, sharing with them about the Lord.

3. Meet on Monday evenings with 4-6 young Christian men for Bible study and discipleship.

4. Lead an outreach based small group of 8-12 church members on Tuesday evenings.

5. Help lead a Boyz Club on Wednesdays with 10-25 inner city and refugee youth, sharing with them about the Lord.

6. Deliver sermons at a church to hundreds of people.

Which of these activities was the most important?

How did Jesus expect a handful of followers to grow into a world of disciples? Jesus had a plan for Kingdom reproduction. His instruction to make disciples in the Great Commission included "[T]eaching them to observe all that I commanded *you*." Mt. 28:20. Each new disciple was to be trained to reproduce just as Jesus had trained His own disciples. We, as Jesus' disciples, are called to make disciples who themselves reproduce.

PRINCIPLE: Jesus called us to make REPRODUCING disciples.

This rolling reproduction yields Kingdom multiplication. In the parable of the minas, the faithful servants only multiplied by five or ten. Five or ten disciples per person - that is sufficient.

It is the statistics of reproduction. We tend to think in large numbers. We want crowds of people. The problem is that big number events don't tend to produce long term disciples. What is the impact of converting 100 people a year versus making 1 reproducing disciple a year?

Making 100 converts in one year is a difficult goal. I certainly have never done it. But if a believer were somehow able to make 100 converts a year for twenty years, there would be 2000 converts.

Making just 1 reproducing disciple a year, though, is a goal that a person might achieve. According to Dr. Keith Phillips of World Impact, if a person can make 1 similarly reproducing disciple a year for twenty years, the total reproduction in those twenty years would be **524,288** disciples. (Source: *The Making of a Disciple*) Kingdom work doesn't necessarily require large crowds. Kingdom work involves exponential reproduction.

Paul clearly understood Kingdom reproduction. He instructed Timothy that "...the things you have heard from me in the presence of many witnesses, these entrust to faithful men, who will be able to teach others also." II Tim. 2:2. In this one verse, Paul envisions four generations of reproduction - from Paul to Timothy to faithful men to others. Paul knew that just a few

19

disciples per person was sufficient.

In my ministry example at the beginning of this section, the most important ministry activity may be discipling 4-6 young men on Monday nights. Because just a few persons meet, those young men have an opportunity to be taught and trained in depth about following Jesus and becoming reproducing disciples. The other activities are important, and they are designed to lead to discipleship, but developing reproductive disciples is where "the rubber hits the road."

PRINCIPLE: Jesus' plan was for exponential Kingdom reproduction - each disciple makes disciples.

A COMPLETE MISSION

How could Jesus leave His disciples with the future of the Kingdom at His departure? How could Jesus expect His disciples to complete the ministry that Jesus began? Jesus brought His disciples into the Kingdom. But just as importantly, Jesus taught His disciples how to make disciples. Jesus knew those twelve assured the future of the Kingdom IF they would obey Him and work using principles of Kingdom reproduction.

Part of our mission is to bring lost souls into the Kingdom of God. But our mission is far from complete at that point. Our mission is not complete until those persons have the ability themselves to disciple others - to instruct and to train others how to reproduce.

PRINCIPLE: Teaching a person how to make a disciple is part of making a disciple.

MEDITATION: "As you have sent Me into the world, I also have sent them into the world." Jn. 17:18.

1. In what ways did Jesus send His disciples, just as the Father had sent Him?

2. What would have happened if Jesus had converted His disciples, but not taught His disciples how to make disciples?

3. Who is Jesus sending today?

REVIEW:

1. Jesus could leave His ministry to His disciples because He had personally discipled them.

2. Conversion is only the beginning of discipleship.

3. Jesus' model was to make REPRODUCING disciples.

4. Jesus' plan was for exponential Kingdom reproduction - each disciple makes disciples.

5. Teaching a person how to make a disciple is part of making a disciple.

LESSON 3 - MODELING

By all accounts, I am not a very good golfer. My evident lack of skill, however, does not deter me from trying to learn the game.

I was at the driving range one day, practicing my game by hitting some golf balls. My usual assortment of shots was on display. On my first swing, I didn't make very good contact. The ball didn't even get airborne. It skittered along the ground - hopping and spinning in reaction to the mounds and clumps of grass which it encountered. This shot went about 100 yards along the ground. It was my classic "wormburner."

On my next shot, the club vibrated as I hit the ball. The ball took off to the right and fluttered in the air briefly. After about 50 yards, though, it veered farther right and dove hard to the ground like a dying quail. This was my shank - a shot mishit off the wrong part of the club.

And then there is the dead slice. The ball ever so briefly leaves the club head straight and initially true, but suddenly makes an almost 90 degree turn in the air and flies along a line perpendicular to the intended direction. On the driving range, the dead slice is the most humiliating shot. Instead of soaring out from the tee, the dead slice turns and travels a direction parallel to the driving range. The ball runs directly in front of the row of other golfers hitting balls. As the ball travels by each golfer, he looks back at where the ball came from as if to say, "What duffer hit that shot?"

When I hit a dead slice, the heads of the golfers lift like a line of dominoes, and they all stare in my direction. Naturally, I turn and look around too, as if someone behind me hit that clanker. This ruse would work except that I am positioned on the end of the range and there are no golfers behind me. The other golfers look at me, shake their heads pityingly, and then go back to hitting balls.

After I hit some more wormburners, shanks and dead slices, a stranger with a golf bag approached me. He had been watching my display of misguided shots. He asked,

"Would you like to hit a golf ball 300 yards? I can help you do that."

I paused for a moment. This offer sounded a little too fantastic to me. I hadn't hit a ball 150 yards yet, much less straight. "No thanks" I said.

The stranger walked away, but I kept a curious eye on him. He set up his bag on the range and began hitting shots. He put his first ball on a tee and swung. Pow! When the stranger hit the ball it sounded like a rifle crack. The ball rose into the air on a soaring trajectory that looked like a frozen rope. It flew 300 yards, straight as an arrow, and landed softly at the other end of the driving range. My mouth involuntarily dropped. He put down another golf ball and hit it. Pow! It made the same sound and had the same result, landing within five yards of his first shot. He hit the third ball, and then the fourth ball. Each one was hit the same way - purely and powerfully. I just shook my head. I had never seen anything like it. He must be a professional.

I almost scrambled to get over to him. "Uh," I sheepishly began, "I might be interested in getting you to help me."

He said "That's fine. First, just watch me for a little bit. Then I want you to show me how you hit a golf ball."

THE IMPACT OF MODELING

What happened on that driving range? I was initially too proud and too stupid to submit myself to the professional's assistance. The stranger modeled a great golf game, though, and that modeling created a desire within me to imitate it. I wanted the ability to hit a golf ball like that stranger. Jesus likewise modeled discipleship to His disciples. What does modeling do?

A. DESIRE - How did Jesus call His disciples? How did He birth the desire to become a follower within the disciples and initiate discipleship?

First, Jesus prayed. Through prayer, Jesus discerned the perfect will of the Father. Lk. 6:12-13 states that Jesus "spent the whole night in prayer to God. And when day came, He called His disciples to Him; and chose twelve of them whom He named as apostles."

Prayer is a requirement for serving God. If we pray, we can hear and fulfill God's will for our lives. If we do not pray, we can not. This book is not about prayer, but suffice it to say that prayer is vital. It is the difference between hitting the mark and completely missing it.

PRINCIPLE: Prayer is the foundation for everything that we do.

Next, when Jesus called His disciples, He modeled effective ministry. Jesus didn't just ask Peter, James and John to follow Him. He first demonstrated the Kingdom of God to them. Jesus demonstrated the authority of the Word by teaching the multitudes from Peter's boat. Lk. 5:3. He then demonstrated the authority of power to Peter and his fellow fishermen whose fruitless toils had convinced them that there were no fish left in the Lake of Gennesaret. They had fished all night and had not caught one fish. But in one cast at Jesus' bidding, the amazed fishermen went from a night of empty labor to boats so full of fish that they began to sink. Lk. 5:4-7. Peter's reaction summed up the impact of Jesus' modeling – "Depart from me, Lord, for I am a sinful man." Lk.5:8. At that point, Jesus issued His call to discipleship.

Effective modeling evokes a comparison. On the driving range, I was left to compare my pitiful shanks with the professional's bombs. People all around us see our character, our lifestyle, our work, our authority and our holiness. The impact of the display of our lives should not be underestimated.

PRINCIPLE: Modeling creates and increases desire to become a disciple of Christ.

B. AUTHORITY - After the disciples had been with Jesus awhile, He called them together and "gave them power and authority over all the demons, and to heal diseases." Lk. 9:1. This commission is a bold one. It isn't every day that someone claims to bestow authority over all demons and diseases. But the disciples didn't question Jesus on this one. Why not?

In the prior chapter, Luke 8, they had just witnessed Jesus in action. With an amazing exhibition of power, Jesus calmed a gale with mere words; cast demons out of a hopelessly insane man - the Gerasene demoniac; healed a woman who had been stricken with a malady for twelve years; and raised a young girl from the dead. The disciples didn't have to ask if Jesus had to ability to give them power over demons and diseases. The disciples knew that Jesus had this authority because they had just seen it demonstrated. Likewise, in the golf example, I realized that the professional could teach me to hit a golf ball because he demonstrated authority over the golf ball and the club.

When authority from God flows, God is at work. The display of this authority proves that God is real and that He is at work through His servants. Over and over, scripture records the response of unbelievers when Kingdom modeling occurred. "When the multitudes saw this, they were filled with awe, and glorified God, Who had given such authority to men." Mt. 9:8.

PRINCIPLE: Modeling demonstrates the authority of God.

C. <u>EXAMPLE</u> - In Acts 9, the authority of God is in full operation through His servant, Peter. In Lydda lived a man named Aeneas. Aeneas was paralyzed, and had been bedridden for eight years. Peter prays for Aeneas, and then issues this command: "Arise, and make up your bed." Acts 9:34.

Arise, and make up your bed? Peter sounds like Aeneas' mother! I would expect him to say "arise and rejoice" or "arise and believe." Where did "arise and make up your bed" come from?

Peter had seen a paralytic healed before. He had a model. In Mark 2, Jesus healed a paralytic carried by four men and let down through a roof. Jesus said, "Arise, take up your pallet and walk." Mk. 2:9-11. Peter was simply following the model that Jesus provided.

Next in Acts 9, a disciple named Tabitha (Dorcas) dies in Joppa. The disciples send for Peter. Peter arrives to a room full of grieving friends. Peter sent all of the people out of the room, knelt down over the body and said, "Tabitha, arise!" Acts 9:39-41. Tabitha opened her eyes and sat up. How did Peter learn to raise the dead in this manner? He had seen Jesus do it this way! In Luke 8, Jesus revived a dead girl. Jesus put everybody out of the room, except Peter, James, John and the girls' parents, and then said "Child, arise." Lk. 8:51-56. Peter learned what to do because he saw Jesus do it.

HOW DO WE MODEL DISCIPLESHIP?

The most influential person in my life? That is a hard description. That person did not have a large or imposing physique. No beauty contest won there. The voice was not booming or resonant. The personality did not command attention. It was not strong or forceful, yet it was not weak. That person was tough and had survived some extreme hardships. Despite the hardships, there was no apparent bitterness. The personality was pleasing - gracious and serving.

The most influential person in my life did not ever hold a position or a title. I don't know of any plaques, awards or prizes received. That person did not hold a job. In fact, that person never held a driver's license, and if that person ever drove a car, I don't know about it. That person did not fit the model for leadership promoted in books about effective leaders.

The talents were not flamboyant or showy. No need for attention was shown. Yet the talents existed and they were immense. You might have to observe awhile to appreciate them fully because the talents were exercised for the benefit of those around that person. The lifestyle was geared to serve others.

The most influential person in my life brought out the best in others. That person rarely said anything negative about anyone. That person saw the positive traits in each individual, and encouraged and emphasized those traits. As a result, other people were encouraged in their gifts and talents, and strove to use them to serve others. The most influential person specialized in healing wounded souls. That person literally saved the lives of numerous hurting and downtrodden individuals, and restored their esteem in the process.

How would I describe the most influential person in my life? Gentle, serving, caring and loving. What was the impact on those blessed enough to be around that person? People wanted to imitate that person. They observed that person's service to them, and wanted to do the same to others, and particularly back to that person. And from what I can tell, they all wanted to do that person's bidding, which was amazing given the fact that person almost never made any demands.

If you want to model discipleship for others, you need Christlikeness within you.

A. If you want to influence another person to grow in Christian character, you need to display Christian character within yourself.

B. If you want to help another person grow in their relationship with the Lord, you need to have a close and abiding relationship with the Lord yourself.

C. If you want to train another person in ministry, you need to be doing that same ministry yourself.

Here is something that I learned from the most influential person in my life: CHARACTER IS CAUGHT AS MUCH AS IT IS TAUGHT.

The second requirement to model discipleship is a relationship with others. You need a forum for discipleship to be modeled. By relationship, I mean long term, long time, close and regular interaction. If you think of the most influential person in your life, chances are good that the person is a family member, roommate or a close friend - a person with whom you spent a lot of time.

As you read the gospels, you realize the vast investment of time and relationship that Jesus made in His disciples, and particularly in Peter, James and John. It was an investment that had eternal consequences.

I was sitting on the back porch with Allie, a person who was close to me personally. Allie had been struggling with a number of personal issues, not the least of which was unbelieving cynicism.

Allie was very bright, but was feeling patronized and unappreciated. Allie began attacking Christians. Christians failed to live like Christians should. In fact, all Christians were hypocrites. They preached one thing, but actually did another.

Allie looked over at me to see the effect of this tirade. Given Allie's mood and the tone of his voice, I decided to keep silent. There was an element of truth in what Allie was saying.

Allie was a little chagrined at my unresponsiveness. So Allie decided to increase the level of attack, and began talking about me personally. I was just like those other Christians that Allie knew. If I really practiced love, I would act differently toward others, and especially toward Allie. I would be more generous, more caring and more understanding. I had failed in my religion or rather my religion had failed me. I was a hypocrite like every other Christian Allie knew.

Once again, Allie looked over at me to see the impact of this attack. I shrugged my shoulders. "I have no defense," I said. "I have failed many times and can only ask God to help me."

Allie shook his head in disgust. He threw down the gauntlet. If I could name just one person who claimed the name of Jesus and who lived as a Christian should, then maybe, just maybe, Allie would believe that there was a God. I was surrounded by Christians, but I knew they were all hypocrites. I couldn't name one person who lived their life as a Christian should.

I paused for a moment. "I can think of somebody close," I said.

Allie snorted and shook his head. "Who?" he demanded.

I said one word. I named the name of the most influential person in my life, a person with whom Allie was also well familiar.

For the first time all evening, Allie paused. The name had impact. He opened his mouth and started to respond, but stopped. He paused again to rally.

Finally, he said, "Well, I would say something because I still think I am right. But I'm not going to. I can't say anything bad about [that person]." Even Allie, in his woeful state, had too much respect for the character shown by the most influential person in my life to demean it.

> PRINCIPLE: Our example outlasts our achievements.

MEDITATION: "He who practices the truth comes to the light that his deeds may be manifested as having been wrought in God." Jn. 3:21.

1. Is there a connection between practicing the truth and being drawn "to the light"?

2. For whom is your life on display?

3. Do your deeds openly show God's workmanship?

REVIEW:

1. Prayer is the foundation for everything that we do.

2. The Impact of Modeling:

    A. Modeling births a desire to become a disciple.

    B. Modeling demonstrates the authority of God.

    C. Modeling shows how to do ministry.

3. Requirements for Modeling:

    A. To talk the talk, a disciple must walk the walk.

    B. A close relationship with others.

    C. Regular and meaningful time with others.

4. Our example outlasts our achievements.

LESSON 4 - TRANSFORMING

I was looking into the eyes of a very angry young man. In his eyes, I saw both hurt and rage. The young man had just cursed me. He didn't only use one or two words. He cursed me violently and vehemently. He cursed me. Then he cursed my wife. Then he cursed my mother. Not just once - repeatedly. He blistered me once - and then he returned to blister me again. He used the foulest words. This tirade wasn't the first time.

Omar was thirteen years old. He was an extremely bright young man. Omar grew up overseas in a different culture and influenced by a different religion. Omar's homeland was a civilized nation, but it had been shattered by a religious civil war. Hundreds of thousands of people died due to fighting, mass executions, starvation and disease. Omar and his family had experienced horrors that no person - much less a young boy - should ever have to see. Even more, after coming to the United States, Omar was subjected to abuse by his own family.

Omar loved to play soccer, and he played it intelligently. He came to our international soccer outreach regularly, but he rarely lasted through the whole session. Omar usually became angry at some one - a teammate, an opponent or the referee. He would blow up and eventually stomp off. On this occasion, I was the referee, and I was the target of his considerable frustration.

Omar was fouled by an opponent, and used inappropriate language. I stopped the game, went over to Omar and cautioned him about his language. Omar looked at me defiantly and said, "Are you [expletive] blind?"

I began the established progression of discipline. I pulled out a yellow caution card, and held it up as I said, "Omar, please calm down."

But Omar was just warming to the task. He began arguing loudly and in the process, intentionally used a word that guaranteed a red card. I just shook my head and held up the red card. I instructed Omar to go to the sidelines.

Under our system of discipline, the first red card meant that a player had to sit out for five minutes. The second red card meant he had to leave the field and could not play for the rest of the day. The suspension after the first red card allowed a player time to cool off. Most players stopped at one red card and reluctantly went to the sidelines, usually making one or two more mild protests on the way to save face.

At the first red card, though, Omar snapped. He began a tirade directed at me. It was a volley of invective full of foul words and personal insults. I held up the second red card and told Omar to leave the field. He adamantly refused, and continued to curse at me.

The occasions when defiance reached this level were very uncomfortable. I didn't have any real power over these young men. Their participation was voluntary. My normal procedure at this point was to use peer pressure. I announced that the game would not continue until Omar left the field. Other players started to urge Omar to leave. He refused, cursing all the while. A number of other players became angry. Eventually they almost physically removed Omar from the field so the soccer could resume.

Omar did not leave the area though. He stood outside the fence during the rest of the afternoon, hurling occasional taunts or insults to anyone who would listen.

When play ended, I cleared the field and carried the equipment to my car. Omar approached me, again cursing me. He directed every hurtful thing that he could at me. I stood there silently, looking into the eyes of a very angry young man.

Finally, I said, "Omar, you can say whatever you want. I'm not going to react. You are not going to get a rise out of me."

Omar paused. His eyes grew big. They showed both surprise and confusion. He looked stunned, as if he was experiencing something new and unusual.

At that moment, I too realized something. Omar was accustomed to cursing adults. Every time he cursed an adult from his culture, he provoked a vehement and often violent reaction. Omar didn't really care about the consequences of his attacks. He had been cursed and beaten for them, but that didn't bother him.

What mattered to Omar was that he was in control. By provoking a response, Omar controlled the reaction of the adult. With his mouth, Omar had power over every person around him. My response to Omar was the first time he had not been able to provoke anger from an adult male. He had lost his control over the situation. It was a new paradigm for him.

Omar was speechless. "Omar," I continued "you need to grow up. You need to learn what it means to be an adult and to control your own feelings and reactions. You need to learn about love and what it means to love people around you."

Omar still looked stunned. He didn't know what to say. After a long pause, he cursed me again. But this time it was more methodical than passionate. He turned and walked away.

I didn't know if I would see Omar again. But I did see him again. A couple of weeks later he came to our Boyz Club - a weekly meeting that we held with international young men for games, fellowship, and sharing. Omar's attitude toward me changed markedly. He started treating me with utmost respect, addressing me as "Coach" and "Sir." I treated him respectfully as well. Omar began attending Boyz Club faithfully. He asked me numerous questions about life and the Lord. He was a bright person and the questions were deep.

Later, we were able to sponsor Omar and take him to Christian camps in the summer. At the time of this writing, Omar is attending church and applying to reputable colleges.

A SEA OF CHANGE

An eye opening experience. A new way of living. The turning point. Jesus' teaching and ministry were dynamic. Wherever He went, for those willing to listen and receive, Jesus changed their lives. Jesus brought transformation. He transformed by example. Then He transformed by proclamation and teaching.

Jesus' proclamation, and the proclamation that He taught His disciples, focused on a central theme. Here are some examples:

1. Mt. 3:1-2 – "John the Baptist came, preaching in the wilderness of Judea, saying, 'Repent, for the kingdom of heaven is at hand.'"

2. Mt. 4:17 – "From that time Jesus began to preach and say, 'Repent, for the kingdom of heaven is at hand.'"

3. Mt. 10:7 - (Jesus to His disciples) "As you go, preach, saying 'The kingdom of heaven is at hand.'"

4. Acts 1:3 – "He also presented Himself alive ...speaking of the things concerning the kingdom of God."

5. Acts 28:31 (the last verse of Acts) - [Paul was] "...preaching the kingdom of God, and teaching concerning the Lord Jesus Christ with all openness, unhindered."

Do you see a pattern here? The phrase "Kingdom of heaven" is used 31 times in the gospels; the phrase "Kingdom of God" is used 51 times (ASV). (Matthew frequently uses the phrase "Kingdom of Heaven"; other gospels use "Kingdom of God.")

The Kingdom of God is a novel concept. It is a paradigm much different than our human existence here on earth. The Kingdom of God is a new experience. It was so foreign to earthly thinking that in order to try to convey its wonder to His disciples, Jesus used parables about the Kingdom of God. "This is what it is like..."

Here are a few principles from those parables:

1. Mt. 13:31-32 – "This is what it is like..." The tiny mustard seed grows into a huge tree and provides a haven for the birds.

PRINICIPLE: The Kingdom of God *grows* (exponentially) and changes its environment.

2. Mt. 13:33 – "This is what it is like..." A little yeast leavens a large lump of bread. The Kingdom of God may start small, but it *spreads*. (It's infectious!) As it spreads, it infiltrates every aspect and every part. The Kingdom of God impacts everything around it.

PRINCIPLE: "Wherever a disciple goes, the Kingdom goes."

3. Mt. 13:44-46 – "This is what it is like..." The pearl and the treasure in the field that are so priceless that everything else is sacrificed in order to obtain them. The Kingdom of God has *surpassing value.*

PRINCIPLE: "It means everything."

Jesus knew that revolutionary transformation was necessary to introduce the Kingdom of God to earth. The mission of that transformation was to advance the Kingdom of God. The means of the transformation was to plant the Kingdom of God into the hearts of men. "The kingdom of God is within you." Lk. 17:21. The result of that transformation was to rescue men from the kingdom of darkness, and make them disciples in a Kingdom of light.

This transformation is occurring daily in our lives and in the lives of disciples everywhere.

PRINCIPLE: The Kingdom of God requires transformation.

INSPIRATION

A testimony: I once went to visit an elderly man who was ailing. I had heard that he wasn't a Christian. He was sitting in a rocking chair on his front porch when I arrived. He kindly invited me to sit with him and we began to talk.

I shared with him about the Lord and quoted scripture to him. Each time I tried to refer to a verse, he quoted the verse back to me more exactly and correctly than I did, often quoting the passage that the verse came from word for word. I realized that the elderly man knew the Bible much better than I did.

I asked him "Have you read the Bible?"

"Oh yes!" he replied. "I have read the Bible many times."

"Have you accepted Jesus as your Savior and Lord?"

"No, I haven't."

I was perplexed. "Why not?"

He turned his head and looked away from me. "I just haven't" he said. "I just don't believe in the Lord."

No amount of sharing or exhorting could persuade him to open his heart to the Lord.

How is the Kingdom of God imparted? It is not sufficient to have good words or even true words. Holy scripture is our guidepost, but quoting scripture alone is not enough. Satan quoted scripture at the Temptation (Mt. 4:6), yet Jesus contradicted what Satan quoted.

Change in the hearts of men is not effected by us. Change in the hearts of men is only accomplished by the Holy Spirit. For words to be effective, those words must be birthed by the Holy Spirit. This dynamic is called inspiration.

Effective transformation occurs when a person filled with the Holy Spirit speaks forth inspired words that cut to the heart of the matter. "[F]or our gospel did not come to you in word only, but also in power and in the Holy Spirit with full conviction..." I Thes. 1:5. These words do not have to be scripture, but they should be consistent with - and not in contradiction to - holy scripture.

Jesus performed marvelous miracles. Scripture, however, records that people marveled as much at Jesus' teaching as His miracles. "[W]hen Jesus had finished these words, the multitudes were amazed at His teaching; for He was teaching them as one having authority, and not as their scribes." Mt. 7:28-29. Words and miracles both have impact because they both are the work of the Spirit.

PRINCIPLE: Words of transformation come only from inspiration by the Holy Spirit.

HOW DO WE IMPART EFFECTIVE WORDS?

When I meet with a small group, I almost always have something prepared to present. Notwithstanding, after prayer, I usually begin the meeting with general discussion, or even open the floor for questions from the group. During this time, I am listening to the words from the group and the heart behind them. I am asking the Holy Spirit to reveal a direction or for a topic to share. More often than not, the sharing is something completely different than what I have prepared for that evening. More importantly, the real sharing comes from someone other than me. My role is not to dominate by lecturing, but to facilitate the move of the Spirit in the meeting!

FULL OF THE WORD

"Do not be anxious beforehand about what you are to say, but say whatever is given you in that hour; for it is not you who speak, but it is the Holy Spirit." Mk. 13:11.

In order to operate in accordance with this direction, a person must be full of the Holy Spirit Who births God's Word within him. The key phrase is FULL OF THE WORD. "Full of the word" means (1) that the mind has studied and meditated on scripture; (2) the Holy Spirit within has illuminated the word to the heart of the believer; and (3) the word has been put into practice by application in the life of the believer. Number (1) means a person knows scripture in their mind. Number (2) means that scripture is part of the heart and mind through inspiration. But numbers (1) and (2) do not mean much without number (3). Number (3) means that the word has been put into practice and that it is part of the life of the disciple. To share it, you need to live it.

One primary purpose of scripture is that "the man of God may be adequate, equipped for every good work." II Tim. 3:16-4:2. If a believer is full of the Word, then that believer is prepared to bring forth the needed word on any occasion. That saint is "instant in season and out of season."

PRINCIPLE: In order to share effectively, a believer must be full of the inspired Word.

PART OF US

Regular (and by regular, I mean daily) Bible study is essential. I studied scripture carefully for many years without public teaching or title. Sometimes this study seemed almost useless or even foolish. But I knew that the Lord was calling me to study and to teach.

During that time, however, I needed the word within me for my own reproof, correction and training in righteousness. II Tim. 3:16. This season of study was important for me to try to incorporate it as a part of my own life. Then after I not only knew it, but also had experienced it, I could begin to impart it.

In college, my girlfriend (who is now my wife) sprained her ankle. She stepped off a curb awkwardly and rolled over her ankle. That evening, she was in tears as she tried to hobble on her swollen ankle. I imagined that it hurt. I tried to sympathize as I could, but I also remember thinking that she seemed to be making an awful big fuss about it.

The next week, I was playing a game of touch football with some friends. The other team was running back a kickoff. I was the last person with a chance to catch the kick returner. Being the competitive person that I am, I lunged forward to try to tag my opponent. I did tag him. But as I stretched to reach him, my right foot came down on top of his rear heel. I felt my ankle turn violently, and I felt something pop.

The next thing I remember, I was on the ground, holding my ankle and writhing in pain. I watched helplessly as my foot swelled until it looked as if a softball had been attached to the side of it. The x-rays were negative, but that was little consolation when the doctor remarked, "This sprain is so bad, it probably would have been better if you had broken it."

The next six weeks were unbridled agony. The doctor said my ankle was initially too swollen to put in a cast. He put a tightly wrapped "pressure boot" on it, and I was on crutches for two weeks. The pain was excruciating, and even the mind bending medications they gave me seemed to do little to diminish it. I could barely sleep at night. After two weeks, the doctor put me in a "walking cast" for another four weeks. Each morning the cast felt loose, but by evening my ankle had swelled inside the cast such that I could feel it

pressing against the plaster sides.

When my girl friend twisted her ankle, I thought that sprained ankles hurt. But after I sprained my own ankle, I KNEW that sprained ankles hurt. I had experienced it.

It is one thing to know something. It is another to experience it as a part of your life. Too many times, I have heard persons share another person's material, or try to teach principles that they themselves had not experienced. Their presentations showed they did not really have a personal understanding of what they were trying to teach.

If you want to teach about outreach, you need to be doing outreach. If you want to share about parenting, you need to be a parent. You need to have experienced the Word in reality in order to tell others how to apply it. Without experience, the words remain only a concept.

PRINCIPLE: It is difficult to teach what you have not experienced. James 3:1.

By the grace of God, there is a redemptive corollary to this principle of experience: Revelation by the Holy Spirit can equate with experience. The Holy Spirit can illuminate a truth to us such that it becomes a part of us as if we had experienced it.

MEDITATION: "Every scribe who has become a disciple of the Kingdom of heaven is like a head of a household, who brings forth out of his treasure things new and old." Mt. 13:52.

1. What is the treasure of a scribe?

2. What do you think "things new and old" means?

3. Jesus said this after He told His disciples a series of parables about the kingdom of heaven. What expectations is Jesus expressing for one who has become a disciple of the Kingdom of heaven?

REVIEW:

1. Jesus' teaching focused on the Kingdom of God.

2. The Kingdom of God requires transformation.

3. Words of transformation come only from inspiration by the Holy Spirit.

4. A disciple must be full of the inspired Word.

5. It is difficult to teach what you have not experienced.

LESSON 5 - TARGETED TEACHING

The stranger walked away, but I kept an eye on him. He set up his bag on the range and began hitting shots. He put his first ball on a tee and swung. Pow! When the stranger hit the ball it sounded like a rifle crack. The ball rose into the air on a soaring trajectory that looked like a frozen rope. It flew 300 yards, straight as an arrow, and landed softly at the other end of the driving range. My mouth involuntarily dropped. He put down another golf ball and hit it. Pow! It made the same sound and had the same result, landing within five yards of his first shot. He hit the third ball, and then the fourth ball. Each one was hit the same way - purely and powerfully. I just shook my head. I had never seen anything like it. He must be a professional.

I almost scrambled to get over to him. "Uh," I sheepishly began, "I might be interested in getting you to help me."

He said "That's fine. First, just watch me for a little bit. Then I want you to show me how you hit a golf ball."

The professional hit some more golf balls. He began to describe each shot before he swung - how far the ball was going to fly; the shape of the shot - straight, bending left or bending right; and whether the ball flight would be high or low. Every time the shot flew just as he predicted. The ball seemed to dance off of his clubs.

I was floored. I began to think, "There is not any possible way that I can do that." The pro started telling me what he was doing on each shot to make the ball react in the way he wanted.

The professional then asked me to hit some balls. A sense of dread - even a sense of helplessness - washed over me. My horrible shots would only increase my humiliation.

As if he sensed my chagrin, the professional said, "Let me explain a few things. First, I didn't ask you to hit some balls to embarrass you. I need to see you hit some balls in

40

order to know how to teach you. I need to evaluate your strengths and your weaknesses so I can see where to start.

"Second, this is no time for pride. Pride does not factor into this process. Your pride will only prevent you from becoming the golfer that you should be. Lose your pride now and never let it hinder you again.

"Most importantly, know and believe that you can be a good golfer. I can help you and equip you to do it. I have done it with other golfers, some of whom were much worse golfers than you are right now. You have the ability to do this."

I took a deep breath and tried to obey him. I began hitting shots - pitiful as they were. And the pro slowly and patiently began teaching me how to hit a golf ball.

The pro gave me numerous lessons. The progress was slow. I had so far to go; it was a complete makeover of my golf life. But my swing gradually improved as I grew in my knowledge of it.

One glorious day after many, many lessons, I hit what seemed like a perfect shot. When I struck the ball it sounded like a rifle crack. The ball rose into the air on a soaring trajectory that looked like a suspended rope. It flew 300 yards, straight as an arrow, and landed softly at the other end of the driving range. I was ecstatic. "Now!" I thought to myself. "Now, I am a golfer!" I imagined I saw a hint of a smile on my teacher's face.

Jesus was the Word of God. Jn. 1:1. He imparted the Word of God. He proclaimed the Word of God, He taught it and He sowed it until it was implanted into the hearts of His disciples. The Word of God emanated from Jesus. The end result was that the Word became a part of His disciples.

Jesus taught His disciples.

RELEVANCE

What should we teach? How did Jesus know what to speak? Every word He spoke was inspired for the person(s) and for the occasion. He cut to the heart of the hearer - to the heart of the matter. That was perhaps the most astounding aspect of Jesus' ministry.

When a person met Jesus, that person had an encounter. And in the course of the encounter, the thoughts and desires of that person's heart were exposed. Jesus peered beyond the symptoms and the disease. He cut to the core issue(s) of that person's life. From the woman at the well (John 4), to the rich, young ruler (Mark 10), to Mary and Martha (John 11), Jesus spoke words of specific application for each life. His words were Words of life to the hearer.

Discerning the heart of an audience is the difference between firing blindfolded with a shotgun, and shooting at the bulls' eye with a rifle. Empathy is a key to effective communication.

> PRINCIPLE: The starting point of teaching is the hearer.
> Spiritual discernment of your audience is essential.

Rom. 10:17 says, "Faith comes from hearing, and hearing by the word of Christ." The Word of God leads to hearing; and the hearing of it leads to faith. We encourage hearing by being relevant to the heart of the hearer.

> PRINCIPLE: Teaching should be relevant to the hearer.

HOW DO WE TEACH?

Over the course of a soccer season we have approximately fifty soccer practices. Through the years, I have written and compiled a whole season of soccer practices - from the first practice to the final practice. This compilation is my coaching book. Each team that I coach does these fifty practices. At the beginning of the season, I can tell you which practice we are going to do on August 19, and which practice we will do on October 29. Without regard to the makeup of the team, or the level of experience or talent, we stick to these fifty practices. Win or lose, play well or play poorly - my next practice is set.

The practices are new to the freshmen. The seniors on the team, of course, are doing the practice series for the fourth time. It doesn't matter how many times they have done it, though. It isn't going to hurt for them to hear the same instruction again, or do the same

drills again. My feeling is that if the practice content is good, the repetition is worthwhile.

Am I a good coach? Am I maximizing the potential of my team and my players?

The truth is that I do not have a practice book. Every practice for every team is different every day. Each team has different personnel with different levels of experience and different talents. Playing one formation may be good for one team, and playing multiple and varied formations may be good for another team. It is necessary that I know my team in order to decide how to teach it.

I determine the content of each practice the night before it occurs. I try to discern exactly what my team needs to learn at that time by observing my team. If we have just played a game, I may see an area of defense that we need to strengthen. The next practice will focus on this area. I have repeated the same drills a number of times through the years when they are applicable. There are many times, however, that I have designed new drills because I believe they pinpointed the exact area of improvement needed.

My practices address the exact need that I discern in my team at that time.

It is unrealistic to expect a static list of fifty practices to apply to every soccer team in every situation. The practices may be wonderful, but that does not mean they are applicable. Yet we often expect the same curriculum to instruct all people. Many congregational models operate on the idea that hundreds or even thousands of people will benefit from hearing one person share the same material - repeatedly. In the words of one sage, "The good or better is often the enemy of the best."

The most meaningful teaching ministry occurs personally - in small groups or one on one. In order to teach effectively, you need to have a relationship with your audience. If you know them - their needs, their culture, their strengths, and their weaknesses - then you have the opportunity to present something that is meaningful to them. Likewise, my golf pro had to see my swing in order to discern where to begin my instruction. Relational instruction helps to facilitate relevance.

I host a Monday night Bible study for international young men. One night, Jorge turned to me and said, "Coach. I like coming to Bible study. I learn a whole lot more here than I do in church."

I reflected for a moment. "Thank you, Jorge, for saying that" I replied. "My guess is that is because of the format and not because of the teacher. In this group, we focus on young men, but a church audience is much broader."

PRINCIPLE: Effective teaching begins with relationship.

DYNAMIC TEACHING

Our teaching must focus on meaningful change for each disciple. We discern the state of each disciple, and help him grow in the Kingdom. Remember the discipleship progression:

CONVERSION > SPIRITUAL GROWTH > TRAINING >RELEASE INTO MINISTRY

(Gospel)   (Christian beliefs)   (Calling)

                    (Personal character)   (Equipping)

                    (Christian disciplines)

                    (Christian witness)

1. If a person needs salvation, teaching should focus on Christ, faith, and the gospel.

2. If a person has accepted the Lord, but needs to grow in Him, teaching should focus on Christian growth and disciplines.

3. If a person is living a Christian lifestyle, but is not active in making disciples, teaching should focus on identifying and developing his call and on training for ministry.

4. If a person is fulfilling his call to ministry, teaching should focus on empowering and encouraging him.

PRINCIPLE: Targeted teaching should further a disciple's growth in Kingdom life.

THE HEART

Victor was a Serbian young man who was raised in an orthodox Christian home. Victor attended Bible Club, and then, as a teenager, he attended Boyz Club. He took part in a foundational Bible study.

Victor was extremely bright. He knew Bible stories and he understood Christian beliefs. His answers were almost invariably correct. Victor participated meaningfully in many studies about Jesus and the gospel. His input was thoughtful and appropriate. When you heard Victor, you felt that he had "it," and that he was well on his way to serving the Lord.

But Victor's life told a different story. Victor seemed to always get into trouble. He stole and he ran away from home regularly. Victor lied often, even when confronted with clear evidence to the contrary. He did stupid and even self destructive things. As an older teenager, he stopped coming to Boyz Club and dropped out of school.

What happened to Victor?

Victor knew the gospel mentally, but the gospel had not transformed his heart. Like Victor, hundreds or even thousands may know about Jesus and agree with His gospel with their mind. But their heart has not been transformed. "This people honors Me with their lips, but their heart is far from Me." Mt. 15:8. Jesus said that you would know them by their fruits. Mt. 7:16.

It is easy to participate in group religious activity, particularly when that activity is not very interactive. Our social nature is inclined toward group functions. Religious participation enhances our self image. It is possible to believe in God with our mind, but not love Him with our heart or our soul. Mk. 12:30. The Holy Spirit has not really penetrated the heart.

Because of this fact, I appreciate the value of personal devotions. Personal prayer and Bible study require initiation by the individual. When a person undertakes private prayer, it is an act that evidences faith. When a person fasts alone, that person is submitting his fleshly cravings to the will of God. Thus, Jesus encouraged His disciples to pray, fast and give in secret. Mt. 6:1-8.

PRINCIPLE: Imparting a devotional life lays a foundation for development of Christian character and Christian witness.

MEDITATION: "Whoever speaks, let him speak, as it were, the utterances of God." I Pet. 4:11.

1. What are the "utterances of God"?

2. How do you think that Jesus fulfilled this command?

3. How can we do the same thing and obey this command?

REVIEW:

1. Jesus discerned the heart of each person that He met.

2. Teaching should be relevant to the hearer.

3. Targeted teaching begins with relationship.

4. Targeted teaching should transform the heart.

5. Imparting a devotional life lays a foundation for development of Christian character and Christian witness.

LESSON 6 - PERSONAL TRAINING

I will never forget my first day in court as a lawyer. My firm had sent me to represent a client on a traffic ticket - one of the simplest matters that a lawyer can handle. In the courtroom, the prosecuting attorney reviewed my case. He then offered me a compromise plea on the ticket.

There I stood alone in the courtroom. I had just finished three years of intense study at a prestigious law school. That school required thousands of hours of lectures, teaching, reading and clinics in order to graduate. And I was an honors graduate, mind you. I had taken and passed the North Carolina State Bar exam in order to obtain a law license. But at that moment in that courtroom, all of that instruction and study meant absolutely nothing. I had no training or experience in traffic court. I had not one clue what to do. It was an extremely forlorn feeling.

Mercifully, an older lawyer realized my predicament. She had overheard the offer. She walked over to me. Without patronizing me, she gently said, "That sounded like a pretty good deal. I think I would probably take it."

Greatly relieved, I turned to the prosecutor. "My client will take the plea," I said. I have never forgotten that attorney or the kindness shown in helping me.

We can see it and we can hear about it. But we really have not learned about discipleship or ministry until we have experienced it.

Instruction is not the same as training. Instruction imparts the knowledge of something. Training imparts the application and use of that knowledge. Sadly, many Christians have been lectured much, but have been trained little.

Jesus modeled effective discipleship. He taught effective discipleship. But His disciples had to learn how to minister on their own. So Jesus trained His disciples.

First, he trained them at His side. Next He sent them out two by two to minister on their own - providing guidance, encouragement and correction all the while. Lk. 9-10.

Our society focuses on numbers. We gauge the success of an event or a program by how many attend or how many participate.

It is not so in the Kingdom of God. Success in the Kingdom of God is not measured just by numbers. If Jesus was driven by numbers, He would have wanted His healings to be broadcast worldwide. Instead, He gave strict orders on numerous occasions to keep marvelous miracles a secret. Mk. 1:44; 5:43; 9:9. Why did Jesus give such limiting instructions?

Jesus knew His core earthly mission was to transform a few men into disciples of the Kingdom. It is hard to train a huge number effectively, so Jesus concentrated His efforts on twelve men. He wanted quality. There is not much glory in focusing on just a few persons, but the impact can be huge. If you are interested in the glory of your own ministry, you need to serve a different Master.

> PRINCIPLE: Success in the Kingdom of God is measured by real impact.

One glorious day after many, many lessons, I hit what seemed like a perfect shot. When I struck the ball it sounded like a rifle crack. The ball rose into the air on a soaring trajectory that looked like a suspended rope. It flew 300 yards, straight as an arrow, and landed softly at the other end of the driving range. I was ecstatic. "Now!" I thought to myself. "Now, I am a golfer!" I imagined I saw a hint of a smile on my teacher's face.

I didn't ask my teacher about it, but I had to take this swing to the golf course. I snuck out the next day to play eighteen holes. Confidently, I stood on the first tee with the wind in my hair. I teed up the ball and hit it perfectly. The ball soared into the air straight and true.

But there were two factors for which I had not accounted. First, the wind was blowing from right to left and blew the ball a few yards to the left. Second, the fairway sloped from right to left. When the ball landed, it bounded further left and ran into the rough that lined the fairway. The ball settled into the long, thick grass, and sunk down.

When I reached my ball to hit my second shot, I looked at my ball. It was nestled in a lie that could only be described as gnarly. I had a problem. On the driving range, there were only perfect lies. I didn't know how to hit from deep rough. After selecting a club, I swung at the ball. The grass behind the ball grabbed the hosel of my club and the ball dove hard right. It flew straight into a sand bunker near the green.

Now I had another problem. In all my lessons, I had never hit a ball from a bunker. I tried to hit the ball with my sand wedge, but I might as well have used a pail and a shovel. It took me three shots to get the ball out of the bunker. The third shot only left the bunker because I hit the back of the ball and skulled it. It spurted out of the sand, over the green, and into the lake on the other side.

And that is how my day went. On a driving range, there is a flat surface, neatly mown grass and an open landing area. On the golf course that day, I was hitting from uphill lies, downhill lies and side hill lies. I was hitting from thick grass, long grass or no grass. I was hitting from the sand, the woods and the mud. It was a disaster. My discouragement was immense, almost as deep as when I was hitting shanks, wormburners and dead slices.

At my next lesson, I confessed to my teacher that I snuck out to play a round. He had a wry smile on his face as I told him of the catastrophic results. "I tell you what," he said, "let's work on your swing a little bit more, then I'll go with you to the golf course. I'll show you how to hit those different shots, then I'll let you hit them until you learn them."

And that is exactly what he did. Side by side, playing round after round together, he taught me how to play the game of golf.

I thought my golf lessons taught me how to play the game of golf. In fact, they only taught me how to swing a golf club. The application of that swing to a golf course was a different matter.

My golf instructor knew that instruction alone was not sufficient. He knew that we needed to play together for him to show me how to play the game of golf. Jesus likewise ministered together with His disciples and then sent them out two by two.

The early apostles understood and followed this same model. Most long term ministry was performed by teams - Peter and John; Barnabas and Paul; Paul and Silas; Barnabas and Mark; Paul and Timothy. There are many reasons to minister in tandem. The training received by joint ministry is one of the most important reasons.

PRINCIPLE: The best training method is partnering together in ministry.

A HEART TO ENCOURAGE

Celebrity conversion is never easy. When a prominent sinner becomes a prominent saint, it is so hard to handle the pressures - and to experience the rejection. His old friends shunned him and turned against him. His new "friends," the Christians, were disbelieving that a noted sinner could make such a remarkable change. For the most part, they rejected him as well.

Because of his new beliefs, he couldn't work in his old job. But he survived the initial challenges with his faith intact, relying on the grace he had received. He grew in the Lord. Yet there were dreams, visions and the gospel to which the Lord called him. But these visions just didn't materialize. He found himself back in his hometown - almost relegated, it seemed, to comparative obscurity. He was perhaps even languishing - until the call came.

The call didn't come dramatically. It came in the person of an older saint - a saint that had a heart to mentor and to encourage others in their ministry. This older saint was talented and he himself was the leader in a great move of God. But he saw a place for the younger Christian - a need for the talents and gifts that he had. So the older saint left the revival for a time and went to the younger Christian's hometown. He sought the younger Christian, and convinced him to come work in the revival. And the rest, as they say - the rest is history.

"And Barnabas left for Tarsus to look for Saul; and when he had found him, he brought him to Antioch. And it came about that for an entire year they met with the church, and taught considerable numbers; and the disciples were first called Christians in

This story is about a young Paul. But it is even more about Barnabas. Barnabas had a heart for others. His real name was Joseph. But he imparted such inspiration that the early church called him “Barnabas” - which means the “son of encouragement.” Acts 4:36-37.

Barnabas especially had a heart for young Christians. When other Christians were skeptical about Saul and his conversion, and even afraid of him, it was Barnabas that stood alongside Saul as a brother, and introduced him into the fellowship of the apostles. Acts 9:26-27.

Barnabas saw the gifts in Saul. Thus, he reached out again to him when Saul was home in Tarsus. Barnabas brought him to Antioch to help the church there. They stayed in Antioch for a year - ministering together.

In response to a prophetic word by Agabus, Barnabas and Saul then were sent on a relief mission to Judea - ministering together. Acts 11:29-30. After the mission was fulfilled, they returned to Antioch with another young man for whom Barnabas cared - his cousin, Mark. Acts 12:25.

Next, in response to a call by the Holy Spirit, Barnabas and Saul left on the “First Missionary Journey” - ministering together. Acts 13:1ff. Careful study of the dynamic between Barnabas and Paul on the First Missionary Journey is instructive. Barnabas was the more mature Christian. After the miracle in Lystra, the amazed townspeople tried to worship Barnabas and Paul as gods. Barnabas is the one that the townspeople identified as Zeus, the chief of the gods. Acts 14:12. Barnabas was obviously the leader of the team.

Paul was identified as Hermes, “because he was the chief speaker.” Now Barnabas was a fine speaker in his own right. But he deferred and allowed Paul to do most of the speaking on that trip. Barnabas understood what it meant to permit a younger minister to exercise his gifts and to develop them.

THE IMPACT OF PARTNERSHIP TRAINING

What impact did this partnership in ministry have on Saul? With assistance and encouragement from Barnabas, Saul grew from a local worker in his hometown into Paul, the worldwide apostle and missionary that the Lord intended! Paul also acquired the vision to train and mentor younger disciples. Consider the list of persons that Paul later called his "co-workers" (Greek: *sunergoi*):

Prisca - Rom. 16:3

Aquila - Rom. 16:3

Urbanus - Rom. 16:9

Timothy - Rom. 16:21

Apollos - I Cor. 3:9

Titus - II Cor. 8:23 ("partner and coworker")

Epaphroditus - Phi. 2:25 ("brother and coworker and fellow-soldier")

Euodia - Phi. 4:2-3

Syntyche - Phi. 4:2-3

Clement - Phi. 4:2-3

Aristarchus - Col. 4:10-11

Mark - Col. 4:10-11; Phil.1:24

Jesus Justus - Col. 4:10-11

Philemon - Phil. 1:1

Aristarchus - Phil.1:24

Demas - Phil.1:24

Luke - Phil.1:24

THE END OF THE PARTNERSHIP

After the completion of the First Missionary Journey, the partnership of Barnabas and Paul came to an end. Barnabas, who had a heart for younger men, wanted Mark to go with them on a second journey. Paul did not want to take Mark because Mark had turned back on the first trip. Paul took Silas; Barnabas took Mark; and Paul and Barnabas went their separate ways. Acts 15:36-41.

A mentoring partnership may need to end at some point. When the goals have been accomplished; when the student has grown; and when the mentor has taught him what he needs to know, then it may be time to move forward separately. From Paul's perspective, he was now ready to take and train young ministers himself. In the next chapter, Paul meets Timothy - a young man with whom Paul will have a deep and loving ministry partnership. Acts 16:1-5. Barnabas went together with another coworker, Mark.

MEDITATION: "Pick up Mark and bring him with you, for he is useful to me for service." II Tim. 4:11.

1. Why do you think Paul later found Mark useful for service?

2. How do you think Mark felt when Paul insisted that he and Barnabas should not "take him along" a second time (Acts 15:38)?

3. What impact do you think Barnabas had on the life of Mark, who went on to author a very important book of the Bible (the Gospel of Mark)?

REVIEW:

1. Lecture imparts knowledge. Training imparts the application and use of that knowledge.

2. Success in the Kingdom of God is measured by real impact.

3. The best training method is partnership together in ministry.

4. The most effective trainers are "co-workers" in the Kingdom.

CONVERSION > SPIRITUAL GROWTH > TRAINING > RELEASE INTO MINISTRY

MODELING   TARGETED TEACHING   PERSONAL TRAINING

TRANSFORMING   **CALL**

LESSON 7 - THE IMPORTANCE OF CALL

I was simply scared. It was cold and darkness was falling. I was in strange neighborhood, preparing to knock on a strange door in order to introduce myself to strange people. My life was not in danger, but my psyche was. I was scared.

A few months before, I had sensed a strong call from God. The call led me to reach out to foreign refugee families. A large number of them had been placed in neighborhoods near our church. I had in my possession "CARE packages" of toiletries and other essential items to distribute to the families. My goal was to develop a relationship with the families and to welcome them to our neighborhood and to our church.

The prospect of knocking on a strange door alone scared me. I wasn't a salesman. Lord knew that! In high school, whenever we had a magazine sales drive, I was too fearful to go knock on doors or solicit neighbors. I paid for 2 or 3 subscriptions out of my own pocket just so I would not turn in a blank sales sheet. I tried door to door sales in college. I failed miserably. Other people had talents for "cold calling." Maybe they even enjoyed it. The personal talents I possessed were neither relational nor conversational.

But now, even conversation was out of the question. These families spoke almost no English. They came from a foreign culture. Their homes smelled funny to me, and their mannerisms were peculiar. I was certain that my own characteristics and aroma seemed every bit as odd to them.

The bottom line was that I felt wholly inadequate. Every contact was different. I didn't know what to say or how to act. I dreaded this moment each and every time I did it.

I could return to my car and go home. A loving wife, two welcoming toddlers, and a warm supper awaited me. These thoughts ran through my mind as I stood on that front door stoop. I shook my head to clear my mind and maybe even try to banish the dread that I felt. I had been called to this ministry. I sighed and braced myself. I slowly raised my

hand to knock on the door...

When a person is called by the Lord, he has a sense of agency - that God has authorized him to act in the realm of his calling. The disciple is not functioning within his own program, but he is representing God to those persons to whom he is called. Paul felt this sense of agency. "We are ambassadors for Christ..." II Cor. 5:20.

A called disciple is an empowered disciple. A called disciple knows he is supposed to work where he is called. He will hang in a ministry long after other disciples have given up and gone home - just as I did when I knocked on the doors of total strangers.

A called disciple has a sense of direction and purpose. God has revealed his function, goals and methods. This leading by God vests an assurance of ministry. It is necessary for effectiveness - for without God's leading, the disciple's work will be in vain.

Most importantly, the called disciple knows that he is working in accordance with God's will for his life. Peace and comfort cover the disciple even in the midst of turbulent circumstances. This disciple truly realizes the meaning of Zech. 4:6 – "'Not by might, not by power, but by My Spirit' says the Lord."

TRAINING AND CALL

Helping a disciple realize his call (or calls) from God is one of the most important parts of training. The Lord has a place and a plan for each of us. "'For I know the plans that I have for you,' declares the Lord, 'plans for welfare and not for calamity to give you a future and a hope.'" Jer. 29:11

Obedience to the Lord's call is the place of peace and fulfillment. A disciple abiding in God's plan for his life is pleasing to the Lord. "And He who sent Me is with Me; He has not left Me alone, for I always do the things that are pleasing to Him." Jn. 8:29.

Pastor Late is an elderly man. I do not know any other person who is so beloved by so many people all over the city. I have spent some time with him and tried to understand why he is so well liked.

One thing that I observed is that Pastor Late has a heart for young people. Many times I have seen him approach a young person and share what he saw in that person. One time when I was a young church member, he came up to me after church and said "I see a shepherding gift in you. You should think about becoming an elder or even a pastor."

Another time, years later, he told me "You have a lot of gifts that I see. You are a strong teacher, but I think that your greatest gift may be discernment."

Both times the words from Pastor Late encouraged me, and maybe even surprised me a little. It wasn't that Pastor Late was always right. He wasn't. It was that he had a heart to encourage, grow and raise up young leaders. This heart was evident in the manner in which he communicated and interacted with others. Many persons consider Pastor Late to be their father in the faith. And that, I believe, is the reason that he is so well loved.

The beginning point for determining the Lord's call is the disciple himself. A call - be it short term or for a lifetime - normally is birthed in the heart of the person called. Pastor Late understood that helping a person discern what the Lord was doing in that person's life, and what giftings the Lord had given to that person were the keys to launching that person into the ministry that the Lord intended for him.

> PRINCIPLE: To help a disciple realize the Lord's direction in his life is one of the greatest services that one disciple can provide for another.

WHAT IS NEEDED TO TRAIN?

The elders of my church asked me to help conduct a Leadership Development Program. We held monthly sessions with presentations and "break out" discussion groups. Topics included the Attitude and Character of a Christian Leader; Spiritual Guidance and the Call to Christian Leadership; Recognition and Use of Spiritual Gifts; the Importance of Relationships; Prayer; and Christian Stewardship. Over the course of the year, much of the instruction and discussion was excellent.

Yet I failed in a significant way. I didn't make the jump from lecture to training. The leaders offered guidance, instruction and encouragement. But I didn't provide action, application or experience. The participants in that program were only partially equipped.

Once a call is identified, training that focuses on the area of call is essential. The goal of the training is to equip the disciple so he has the tools to fulfill the Lord's call in his life.

Training together implies that each and every person (trainer, trainee, or coworker) is actively ministering. Even if I assisted the participants to identify areas of call in the Leadership Development Program, I failed to equip them to fulfill those calls.

Too often, we expect disciples to go and minister after they have only been lectured. It was not so with Jesus. He ministered with His disciples at His side in Luke 8. Next, He sent them on a mission. Lk. 9:1-9. When they returned, He again ministered to the multitudes with His disciples there - welcoming them, proclaiming the Kingdom and healing them. Lk. 9:11.

In order to partner in ministry together, disciples of Christ need an intimate relationship with their coworkers. The key phrase is "coming alongside." To work together effectively, ministry partners need to know each other, their respective gifts and talents. They need to understand the vision that each person has for ministry, and the goals of the joint ministry. The expectations of each person need to be defined. Partners need to know the weaknesses of each person so support can be given at the appropriate time and in the appropriate manner.

THE LAST WISH

My grandparents' next door neighbor, Mr. Tonal, was their lifelong friend. After my grandparents passed away, I went to visit Mr. Tonal in order to honor him and to commemorate the friendship that he had with my beloved Papa and Meme. Mr. Tonal's wife had also passed on. I knew that he missed her and was lonesome.

Mr. Tonal was happy to see me. He insisted that I sit down and talk with him on his front porch. We rocked in the sun and slowly reflected on the past.

Mr. Tonal said, "Well, I'm eighty-six years old now. It seems like time goes too fast...much too fast."

"Are you still going to the prison on Wednesday nights?" I asked. I knew that Mr. Tonal had been visiting the prison faithfully for many years.

"Yes," replied Mr. Tonal, "I'm still goin' to the prison on Wednesday nights. I'm gettin' tired, though. Been goin' to the prison for forty-six years now. Forrr-ty...six...years." Mr. Tonal said "Forty-six years" real slowly as if he couldn't believe it had been that long.

Mr. Tonal continued. "We've done a lot in that ministry. We've had 862 baptisms and 1564 recommitments during that time."

"Wow!" I said. "That is really something."

Mr. Tonal paused. "You know," he reflected, "I don't want that ministry to stop. I wish I could find someone to take my place there."

"How about one of the prisoners that has been paroled? Isn't there anyone that has benefitted from your ministry that participates in it now?"

Mr. Tonal shook his head. "No. I'm not sure why not. I just don't have anybody to take my place." He furrowed his brow. "Maybe Johnny Dale would be interested in continuing that ministry. He came with me to the prison a few weeks ago. Maybe Johnny Dale could do that."

I suppressed a smile. I knew Johnny Dale. Johnny Dale was about 75 years old. He couldn't move around much better than Mr. Tonal. Johnny Dale didn't exactly represent the next generation of ministry.

Mr. Tonal and I talked some more and then I told him good-bye. As I walked back to my family's home place, I thought about what Mr. Tonal had said. Eighty-six years old and in the ministry forty-six years and now - only now is he thinking about training a replacement.

Understand the attitude of a servant leader. If a leader is concerned just about his ministry, he does not possess the attitude of a servant leader. I do not like to hear a Christian talk in terms of "my ministry." The ministry is the Lord's and we do not possess it. In fact, we really can not fulfill His ministry until we have fully submitted our work to Him, and are willing to retain or lose our ministry as He pleases. A leader who is focused on his own ministry will consider another person only in the context of how that other person may help or fit into that leader's particular ministry.

A servant leader supports the ministry call of others. He realizes that grooming other leaders is necessary for an effective ministry to continue. If the call of another is in fact related to the leader's work, by training another to fulfill the same work, the leader multiplies the ministry.

PRINCIPLE: Christian leaders seek to work themselves out of a job.

SHARING RESPONSIBILITY

The great difficulty of training another disciple is that you must allow your coworker to do the work of ministry. You may know how to do it better and more effectively, but training will not occur until your coworker has done the ministry himself. Servanthood is not just meeting the physical and spiritual needs of others. Servanthood is allowing another to grow in ministry by leaving him room to do so.

PRINCIPLE: Training allows the other person to take responsibility.

DEFERENCE

The only manner that Christians can work together effectively is by practicing this verse: "BE SUBJECT TO ONE ANOTHER IN THE FEAR OF CHRIST." Eph. 5:21. Only through an attitude of submission to each other can two work in unison. Are you the older Christian? Are you the mentor and the trainer? Are you the more mature disciple? Then show that you understand this verse. It is essential that you demonstrate submission to your fellow Christian, and allow him to learn and do the work of ministry.

MEDITATION: "He must increase, but I must decrease." Jn. 3:30.

1. John the Baptist spoke these words in reference to Jesus. What was he feeling at that time?

2. Is it ever God's will that our ministry should decrease?

3. In the prior verse, John the Baptist says "And so this joy of mine has been made full." Jn. 3:29. Why did he feel this way?

REVIEW:

1. A called disciple is an empowered disciple.

2. Helping a disciple realize a call from God is one of the most important parts of training.

3. The beginning point for determining the Lord's call is the disciple himself.

4. Training allows the other person to take responsibility.

5. "Be subject to one another in the fear of Christ." Eph. 5:21.

CONCLUSION:

MODELING increases DESIRE.

LECTURE increases KNOWLEDGE.

TRAINING increases ABILITY.

TEAM MINISTRY IS ESSENTIAL

Some benefits of team ministry:

1. Partnership brings encouragement when we need it. Acts 18:27 - Apollos

2. Partnership brings support in ministry. II Tim. 4:11 - from Mark

3. Partnership gives confirmation of direction. II Cor. 8:16-17 - Titus

4. Assistance from others helps pride prevention. Rom. 16:3-4 - Prisca and Aquila (Opposite - III Jn. 1:8-9 - Diotrephes)

5. Partnership covers our weaknesses. Phil. 2:30 - from Epaphroditus.

6. Partnership can correct our blind spots. Gal. 2:11-14 - to Peter and Barnabas

7. Partnership allows coordination of giftings (complementary). Acts 14:8ff. - Paul and Barnabas

8. Partnership allows training and growth. II Tim. 2:2 - Timothy

9. Partnership brings the power of agreement. Mt. 18:19.

10. Common quest breeds comrades.

LESSON 8 - RELEASE

We were at our weekly Boyz Club meeting. Boyz Club was formed as a gathering for teenage international and inner city youth. At Boyz Club, we played games, fostered fellowship and shared about life and the Lord.

The presentations at Boyz Club were sometimes planned. Often, though, the sharing was spontaneous. An incident might happen during a game that needed to be addressed; one of the guys might have an important issue in his life to discuss; or we might invite questions or discussion from the group. The spontaniety gave the Spirit a chance to move with immediacy.

At this particular Boyz Club meeting, we opened the floor for discussion. One of the young men began talking about his goals in life. Then another told about his dreams. We went with the flow, and engaged in a session of "visioneering" - hearing and commenting on the vision for life shared by the Boyz Club members.

One of our leaders turned to me and asked, "David, what goals do you have for your life?" He put me on the spot.

After thinking for a moment, I said, "Most of my goals involve areas of my life that have already seen dreams fulfilled. I always wanted a family. Now that I have one, my goal is to be a good husband and father. I have my own business, so I want to be a good employer. I think that the Lord has called me to areas of ministry, so I want to obey Him and complete them. Most of my personal goals now involve fulfilling responsibilities that I already have, and maintaining areas that are already established."

I paused for a minute. "But there's more. I have dreams for you - the members of Boyz Club. I want you to do the ministry of Jesus. I want you to reach out to the world around you and make disciples for the Kingdom of God. Each person here has a unique calling on your life from God. My hope is that every one of you is able to find that calling from God and that you fulfill it."

I looked around the room. Every person was quiet. The young men looked at me intently. Softly, I said "Let me tell you something else about me and each of you. I want you to go farther than I have. I want you to do more than I have done ...to do greater things. I want you to go more places and reach more people. Please," I continued, "please see the potential in this room that I see. The guys in this room have incredible giftings. The guys in this room can reach thousands of people for the gospel. The potential that is in this room is unlimited."

I was sincere in what I shared at Boyz Club that evening. But as I thought about what I said, I realized that there were implications if I really wanted those guys to reach their full potential - to go farther than I went, and to do more than I did.

IMPLICATION #1 - I AM IN CONTROL

If I was serious about what I shared with those young men at Boyz Club, I realized that I can't control them. If I control them, I limit them. I limit them to my ability. I limit them to my thinking. I limit them to my calling. If I want them only to go as far as I have gone - to only operate as I have operated, then I should say, "Here is how you function. Do it the way that we have always done it. Do it this way... In this situation, always say this..."

But if I restrict those guys to my methods, they will never go farther than I went. If I want them to go farther, I have to release them from my control. I have to allow them to do more things and in a better way.

Perhaps more importantly, if I control them, they will ultimately resent the fact that I imposed my own woeful limitations on them. Control will only be relinquished if a leader is more interested in the success of others than in his own success. "With humility of mind, regard one another as more important than yourselves." Phil. 2:3.

> PRINCIPLE: It takes the heart of a servant leader to give up control in a relationship.

IMPLICATION #2 - DO IT MY WAY

When I coached soccer, I coached a team from a small, private high school. We fielded some good teams, but we didn't play at the highest level.

One day, Adbu approached me. He was one of my better soccer players. He said, "Coach, I may have a chance to play for Freedom High School next year. What do you think about me doing that - you know, with the team and all?"

It was not unusual for good players to ask me about playing for another team. I hated to lose good soccer players. But at times those players had opportunities to compete at a higher level with better teams. Abdu was asking me if I would be upset with him if he left the team next year.

I looked at Abdu and said "I appreciate you asking me. Abdu, you don't owe me anything. You have played hard for two years and really helped this team. I want you to do what is best for you. I have coached you for two years and taught you what I know. Another coach can teach you more than I can. He can show you different things. It is fine for you to play on another team next year if that is what you think is best for you."

If I genuinely want young men to go farther than me, they will need to do some things differently than I do. I can share what I know with them and train them in it. But I can't require them to be confined to my knowledge and my methods. Those young men will need to grow from that foundation and learn new methods in order to surpass me.

But it is not just a matter of improvement. Each of those guys has a different personality than I have with different traits. They need freedom to approach people differently in accordance with their gifts. Different understanding, different methods and different approach may mean better understanding, better methods and a better approach. If those young men are going to do the work of ministry better than I did, they need freedom to do it differently.

IMPLICATION # 3 - LEARN FROM ME

If I want the young men to go farther than I do, they need new revelation. "For all who are being led by the Spirit of God, these are sons of God." Rom. 8:14.

To understand and fulfill the call that the Lord has on your life, the disciple needs to learn how to be led by God. The disciple needs revelation for his life - a revelation that is different from me or from anyone else. Whom to reach, where to go, how to do it, what to say... What I know is limited and it is primarily intended for me. But the Holy Spirit will reveal so much more to those young men.

Jesus understood the disciples' need for this revelation. He gave them a promise of a "Helper" - the Holy Spirit. "But the Helper, the Holy Spirit, whom the Father will send in My name, He will teach you all things..." Jn. 14:26.

THE EXAMPLE OF JESUS

Saxon was a close friend and accountability partner. I had lunch with him weekly. Saxon was one of the church leaders. He had a heart for missions, and had led a number of short term missions teams.

During one meal, Saxon was bemoaning the restrictions that he experienced in ministry within our church. At times it felt almost like "being handcuffed" or "being put in a strait jacket." Yet when Saxon went on the mission trips, there was a free release into ministry. Coming home was almost like a "let down."

I asked him "Saxon, why do you think that is? What is different between a missions trip abroad and ministry here at home? You are the same person in both places."

Saxon thought for a moment. "Well," he said, "when we go on a trip, we have carefully defined goals. These goals are common goals, and they seem to override any personal differences."

"Also, we are careful to be Spirit led on these trips. We are seeking God's will continuously. We are strongly focused on doing exactly what He wants."

"Finally, each person is released to minister in their gifts. Each person is released to fulfill their potential such that there is a freedom in ministry."

Release leads to freedom in ministry. Release is empowerment. The bottom line is that if

I want other disciples to go farther than me, I have a price to pay. At some point, I have to release them from the confines of my personality and my paradigms.

Jesus understood about the necessity for this release. Shortly before He left them, Jesus told His disciples "It is to your advantage that I go away..." Jn. 16:7.

If I had been one of Jesus' disciples, that statement would have stunned me. "How can it be to my advantage that you go away, Jesus? I will never be closer to God. You are God. You have full revelation. You know what to do in every situation. You are 'the man.' There will never be a greater!"

-But if Jesus doesn't go, the disciples stay in their comfort zone, dependent on His fleshly presence.

-If Jesus doesn't go, the disciples will not be who they were meant to be. They will never fulfill their calling. They will never undertake and fulfill the responsibility of the Kingdom.

-If Jesus doesn't go, the disciples will not be released to accomplish their ministry under the guidance of the Holy Spirit.

Think for a minute of the disciples in the Gospels - bumbling, well-intentioned, but often misguided. "'Rabbi, it is good for us to be here; and let us make three tabernacles, one for You, and one for Moses, and one for Elijah.' For he [Peter] did not know what to answer; for they became terrified." Mk. 9:5-6.

Next, think of the disciples in Acts - confident, empowered, and bold to proclaim. "Now as they observed the confidence of Peter and John, and understood that they were uneducated and untrained men, they were marveling, and began to recognize them as having been with Jesus. And seeing the man who had been healed standing with them, they had nothing to say in reply." Acts 4:13-14. Jesus knew what release meant for His disciples.

Those disciples had been discipled by a Person who defined the attitude of a servant leader. Jesus desired for His disciples to do greater things. "Truly, truly, I say to you, he who believes in Me, the works that I do shall he do also; and greater works than these shall he do; *because I go to the Father.*" Jn. 14:12.

How could the disciples do greater works than Jesus? What does going to the Father have to do with those works? It is hard to understand all that verse means. Does "greater works" mean greater miracles? Maybe, but what miracle is greater than raising a person from the dead? Is a sign or a wonder the greatest work? Or is the greatest miracle the miracle of faith?

Jesus valued disciples. Think of "greater works" in terms of making disciples. Jesus' disciples went a farther distance than Jesus did. They ultimately reached more people than Jesus did. Jesus was called to the lost sheep of Israel. He sent the disciples to the whole world when He went to the Father. Could Jesus have been thinking of the Kingdom - its expansion and growth - when He promised "greater works"? Could He be thinking of the number of disciples they would make?

This promise is not limited to the twelve apostles. It is a promise to "he who believes in Me." Who is working "greater works" of Jesus today? Who has this responsibility today?

Side by side, round after round, my friend, the professional, showed me how to play golf. He showed me how to hit high shots and low shots; straight shots and bending shots. He showed me how to hit from short grass and from tall grass; from mud and from hardpan; from bunkers and from waste areas. He taught how to play in the wind and in the rain; in the heat and in the cold. His patience was extraordinary, but he knew that it was important that I be the one to hit the shots. Months turned into years.

One day, after we finished a round in which I had played extraordinarily well, he paused and looked at me, then he looked far off as if he was searching to find something. "It is time," he said. "You are ready to play on your own. Remember what you have learned, and come back to see me if you need me."

Then he shook my hand and started to walk away. He stopped and turned. "One more thing, don't ever give up."

I took my game to the course and began to participate in matches. I initially struggled. Shots that were easy in practice became extremely difficult when they counted. It is one thing to play the game. It is another to compete. When what you do really matters - when it has real impact - the pressure mounts. Once again, I had to grow. I had to learn not just how to play, but I had to learn how to win.

MEDITATION: "You give them something to eat!" Lk. 9:13.

1. Jesus spoke these words to His disciples prior to feeding the five thousand. Was Jesus serious?

2. How did His disciples feel about this command?

3. Have you ever felt that the Lord has asked you to do something far beyond your ability?

REVIEW:

1. To reach his full potential:

    A. A disciple must be released from control.

    B. A disciple must be free to use different methods.

    C. A disciple needs his own revelation.

2. Jesus knew that it was beneficial for Him to release His disciples into ministry.

3. A leader must be willing to release disciples into their ministry.

LESSON 9 - OUR HURDLES

I once heard a young person report about a recent mission trip. She was zealous, perceptive and intelligent. Here is what she shared about the countries she visited:

"We went to Scotland first. The city we stayed in was dingy and the weather was dreary. The people that I talked with seemed downcast - almost depressed. Maybe it was the weather, but everyone acted as if they led pained lives. Lonesomeness was rampant. The society was technologically advanced, but I sensed a loss of community. There was a pall over the whole area.

"Next we went to Germany. The Germans that I met were rigid and hard people. They didn't want to listen to any sharing about the Lord. It was as if they thought what they wanted to think - whether or not it was right. Their minds were made up and their hearts were set in stone. I am not used to the hardness that I experienced in Germany.

"When I returned to the United States, I realized that people are much more upbeat and much freer. They are distracted, though. Americans have a lot of possessions and toys. Their lives are geared toward acquiring more possessions and bigger toys. Americans are so busy entertaining and amusing themselves that they don't have time to hear the Word."

After the service, I approached the young lady and said "Thank you for your sharing. It was very perceptive. Did you realize that in each country you described a type of soil in Jesus' parable of the sower?"

The young lady paused for a moment and looked at me quizzically. "Really?" she asked. "What do you mean?"

"Well," I said, "when you portrayed the people in Scotland, you described the soil that was..."

The parable of the sower is one of Jesus' most important parables about the Kingdom of God. (Mt. 13; Mk. 4; and Lk. 8). In the parable, Jesus describes a sower spreading seed. The seed falls on four different types of soil. Jesus tells us what occurs when the seed falls on each ground.

Jesus later tells His disciples that the seed is the Word of the Kingdom. Mt. 13:19. The soil is the heart of the hearer. Mt. 13:19; Lk. 8:12. The sower throws out the same seed, but different results occur depending on the heart of the hearer. This parable gives us insight into the human heart and its reaction to the Word.

THE HARD GROUND

"And as he sowed, some seeds fell beside the road, and the birds came and devoured them." Mt. 13:4

Hard ground resists the penetration of seed. Why is the ground hard? It is beside a road and has been trampled upon by the many people walking there. This ground is like the sidewalk in an era before sidewalks.

This soil represents hearts that have been trampled, hurt and broken. They are scarred and closed as my friend experienced in Scotland. Because of pain and fear of more pain, these hearts can not open up and receive the Word. The pain blocks penetration. Jesus says that these hearts do not understand the Word, so Satan comes and snatches it away.

Understand why hurt lives resist the gospel. Hurt lives are full of distrust and fear. They have not experienced love and can not receive love. For example, hurts inflicted by an abusive earthly father make it extremely difficult to understand the love of our heavenly Father.

Catherine R. was one of those hurt souls. Catherine's husband rejected her and left her. He then divorced her. Catherine began a downward spiral emotionally and financially and, in the process, became alienated from her family. She had almost no friends and she was destitute when she met Meme. Meme was a stranger, but Meme opened her home to Catherine.

It wasn't that Catherine was an unfriendly or antisocial person. In fact, she was too friendly. She tried to help in any way that she could, almost throwing herself at you. Catherine had such a need for belonging...such a craving for acceptance, that she tried way too hard to be helpful. She smothered other people with herself. It was almost repulsive.

Then, when Catherine sensed a rejection of her good intentions from other people, it only injured her esteem more. Catherine was a wounded soul. But Meme specialized in wounded souls.

Meme took Catherine under her wing. She knew that Catherine needed to be busy and to do things that she could feel good about. Meme put Catherine to work cooking, cleaning, sewing and baking. Meme worked with her and praised her successes. During the next few months, Meme encouraged Catherine, listened to her, and counseled her. Meme prayed for her, and Meme prayed with her, sharing the love of God tangibly and intangibly.

Catherine's personal esteem slowly grew. Her self-destructive habits began to diminish. She received balm for her wounds and hope for her future. Catherine recovered to the extent that she was able to move out and live on her own. Yet she knew that if she needed support or a listening ear at any time, she had a friend in Meme that was faithful, caring and available.

Meme prominently displayed a framed statement in her room that inspired her. It also described her calling. The statement read:

> ## PEOPLE NEED LOVE THE MOST WHEN THEY DESERVE IT THE LEAST

Hope exists for the trampled heart. Packed soil can be loosened and carefully restored. God can heal a wounded soul through digging deeply and kneading it - clump by clump. This soil can be cultivated and softened through ministry, healing, and abundant love. Then, only after this loving cultivation, the soil is able to receive the Word.

Ministry to hurt lives is difficult and strenuous. It is time consuming. It requires patience and understanding. Hurt lives are dysfunctional. Hurt lives can negatively impact the persons around them. In reaction to the pain, wounded persons can be abrasive and lash out erroneously against the very persons who love them and are trying to help them. But love "bears all things, believes all things, hopes all things, endures all things." I Cor. 13:7.

ROCKY PLACES

I had a friend, Matt, with whom I shared about the Lord. He did not believe, and he made that fact very clear in our discussion.

The sower sows the seed. That sowing is his duty. He does not cause the seed to grow or bear fruit, he only sows. He sows on good soil and he sows on bad soil. As Paul described, "I planted, Apollos watered, but God was causing the growth." I Cor. 3:6.

Believing that only God can birth faith, I left the result to Him. I often encouraged friends who did not believe simply to ask God, if He existed, to reveal Himself to them. If a person was willing to make that request, I resolved to let God respond as He saw fit in His mercy.

When Matt expressed his lack of faith, I challenged him in that regard. "Matt," I said, "I respect your opinion, and I don't want to argue with you. I would only request that you ask God, if He is real, to reveal Himself to you. By doing that, you are open, and the rest is up to Him if He is there."

Matt looked at me for a minute. He shook his head slowly. "You know, David," he said, "I don't think I can do that. I just don't believe that there is a God."

We talked a little more and then I left. As I walked away, I was somewhat stunned. How could anyone be so close minded? I didn't ask him to accept God or even agree that God existed. He was not even open to the possibility of a God.

"And others fell upon the rocky places, where they did not have much soil; and immediately they sprang up, because they had no depth of soil. But when the sun had risen, they were scorched; and because they had no root, they withered away." Mt. 13:5-6.

The rocky ground does not have rocks interspersed on good soil. The rocky area has a thin layer of soil on top of a solid shelf of rock. There is no depth underneath the surface. Mt. 13:5.

The amazing fact about this ground is that it looks like good soil. In fact, the thin layer of soil is fertile as it may initially receive the Word. Mt. 13:5. On the surface, this heart is indistinguishable from a faithful heart. This person is soft, gentle and "normal" - even churchgoing. This facade enables this person to function socially and religiously, but it is deceiving. Underneath, the core of the heart is hard and rigid as my friend experienced in Germany. It is really a heart of stone - a heart of unbelief.

When the plants initially grow in this soil, the sun scorches them. Lk. 8:6 says they are scorched because they receive no moisture. Sun is good for plants and even necessary for photosynthesis. But moisture is also necessary. The problem with this soil is not a lack of moisture. It receives plenty of rain. The problem is the rock underneath rejects the moisture and can not receive it or retain it.

Presentation of the Word to this heart may at first seem successful. The gospel may be accepted mentally or even emotionally, but the Holy Spirit has not penetrated the heart. The hard heart rejects the Holy Spirit.

The burning, radiant sun brings this fact to light. Faced with adversity, or even just exposure, the lack of faith becomes evident. This hardness of heart is the most difficult. It refuses to submit to God, and truly worships only one being - itself.

THE BRIAR PATCH

"And others fell among the thorns, and the thorns came up and choked them out." Mt. 13:7.

This soil is quality soil. It is soft and it is fertile. Seed and water penetrate it, and the good seed flourishes. As my friend experienced in the United States, though, the soil is not pure.

The soil contains other seed that hinders the good plants. These seeds are the "worries and riches and pleasures of this life." Lk. 8:14. This spiritual walk began well, but became distracted by other desires and attractions which block out the growth of the good seed. This heart is a briar patch – choked by possessions, amusements and entertainments.

We have worked with a community of refugees who were persecuted for their Christian faith. We have heard many heartbreaking stories about loved ones who were jailed and tortured or who died for their faith in Christ. This steadfastness is admirable.

When these refugees arrive in the United States, they enter a foreign culture. The parents and elders of the community strive to preserve the traditions and faith of the community. This fact presents a dilemma for their children. The children want to belong to the family and the community, but also want to adapt and meld into American civilization. The children don't want to "stick out like a sore thumb" at school, and they are attracted by the entertainment, pleasure and luxury that American culture offers.

As the parents sense their children drifting from their culture, they become stricter with their children, and even violent. Many children rebel against this harshness. In their desire to experience American lifestyle, the children not only reject their parent's culture, they also reject their parent's faith. They drift away from the Lord.

Thus, what the enemy could not do to one generation through adversity, he accomplishes with another generation through enticement.

The good news is that the thorny soil can be redeemed. Thorns can be removed and give good seed a chance to grow. It may be a painful process as thorns puncture. And it may be a lifelong process, as some seed germinates early and other seed germinates later. But it can be done.

"Therefore, putting aside all filthiness and all that remains of wickedness, in humility receive the word implanted, which is able to save your souls." James 1:21. For the implanted Word to grow, we must put aside all corruption (thorns) and receive it with meekness (no stone).

GOOD GROUND

"And others fell on the good soil, and yielded a crop, some a hundredfold, some sixty and some thirty." Mt. 13:8.

This soil is rich, deep and fertile. It is pure and untainted for growth. It hears the Word; receives it; and soaks up the rain of the Spirit for growth. This soil is the type that we want to be. Hearts that receive and grow.

The parable of the sower is instructive for the sower of the Word. It helps us understand the types of hearts that hear the gospel and discern the heart of recipients.

If there is initial resistance to the Word, is it due to prior hurt? Or is it due to hardness of heart? The value of relational sharing is demonstrated because a closer relationship will assist the discernment. We further understand that acceptance of the Word alone is not sufficient. Just because the Word is initially received or even grows a little does not mean the Word has fallen on good soil. Discipleship is necessary to see the true result of the planting.

This parable is also instructive to help us discern our own hearts. How do we react to the Word? Are we resistant due to pain or pride? Are we tenderhearted and receptive, but not truly productive because our hearts are not pure?

MOST IMPORTANTLY...

This parable is not just about sowing the seed or receiving it and growing. THIS PARABLE IS ABOUT FRUITFULNESS. Good soil is fruitful soil.

Jesus is not only teaching us about hearts that are or are not receptive to the Word. Jesus is teaching us about hearts that are (or are not) fruitful as a result of the Word! The seed was initially received by the rocky soil and by the thorny ground. BUT it was not fruitful. Good soil is fruitful soil! Jesus is telling us the reasons why the seed was not fruitful. If your life is not fruitful, look at your heart.

Wounded souls (trampled soil beside the road) are reluctant to spread the Word because of a fear of rejection. "I am afraid to testify to strangers." Fear of God is the remedy for fear of man.

A person who has fundamental unbelief (rocky soil) is not going to share the Gospel. He doesn't really believe the Gospel even if he outwardly has accepted it. His unfruitfulness evidences a basic lack of faith.

Finally, distractions and pleasures (thorny soil) prevent us from doing the work of the Lord. "I don't have time to go out and do it." Are you concerned with the kingdom or with the world? Will the treasure for which you labor last into eternity, or will it fade away? "They are choked with worries and riches and pleasures of this life, and *bring no fruit to maturity*." Lk. 8:14.

After the Lord called me into outreach ministry, I received a telephone call from a fellow church member. She asked me to help in a specific area.

I thought about my situation at that time. I held a full time job. At home we had two small children and another one on the way. I was also playing golf - a game that I really loved - two times a week. I studied my life and decided that I did not have the time to do it. I called her back and said, "No."

What a fool! As I look back at that person that said "No," I think "What a fool!"When I compare what I do now to what little I did then, I shake my head. Now I have outreach events 3 or 4 times each week. I am teaching and discipling numerous persons. There is prayer and study daily. The person that said "No" was simply uninformed and ignorant.

WHAT A FOOL! When I think of the benefit that I receive from the work of the Kingdom, I realize the foolishness of my response. The fullness of my life is not measured in time or in effort. The fullness of my life is measured in grace, fulfillment and focus. I am daily strengthened by the work of the Lord that occurs around me and within me.

The crucial issue is one of maturity. Maturity in the parable of the sower is gauged by fruitfulness, not by growth. Our fruitfulness demonstrates that the Word of the Kingdom has truly been received into our hearts. Is it possible to believe in the Lord, and even grow in the Lord, and yet still be counted as worthless? "'Behold, for three years I have come looking for fruit on this fig tree without finding any. Cut it down! *Why does it even use up the ground?'* And he answered and said to him, 'Let it alone, sir, for this year too, until I dig around it and put in fertilizer, and if it bears fruit next year, fine; but if not, cut it down.'" Lk. 13:7-9.

The Lord does not desire to cut us down. He wants us to be fruitful!

MEDITATION: "For ground that drinks the rain which often falls upon it and brings forth vegetation useful to those for whose sake it is also tilled, receives a blessing from God; but if it yields thorns and thistles, it is worthless and close to being cursed, and it ends up being burned." Heb. 6:7-8.

1. What type of soil is within you?

2. What does the fruit that your life has yielded show about your heart?

3. How can your life be more fruitful?

REVIEW:

1. The types of soil in the Parable of the Sower are different conditions of the heart.

2. The fact that the Word is initially accepted does not mean it will remain.

3. Good soil is FRUITFUL soil.

4. Maturity in the Kingdom of God is gauged by fruitfulness, not by growth.

LESSON 10 - SPIRITUAL HEALTH

I have here a pill bottle, and I want to give a dose from it to each of you. When you take a pill from this bottle, here is what you experience: The feeling that you have when you participate in the work of God.

When you hear from God and obey what you have heard from Him, you see Him work through that obedience. Because you have seen Him work, you experience God. You have the knowledge that you are in His perfect will and plan for your life. The feeling is complete peace; deep fulfillment; enriched faith; and joyous pleasure.

One reason that I want to give this pill to you is the response that you would have to that feeling. Your reaction would be: "I don't want ever to do anything else. I don't want ever to be anywhere else. I don't want ever to feel anything else. I want always to remain exactly where I am - in God's perfect will."

In John 4, Jesus meets and ministers to a Samaritan woman at a well. He shares the Gospel with her. The woman receives His word and joyfully runs back to her city to share the good news. Through her proclamation, many other townspeople came out of the city and met the Master. "And many more believed because of His word." Jn. 4:41.

But this story is about a lot more than just encounters. This story is about food and water.

JESUS IS THIRSTY

Jesus is thirsty. He and His disciples have been on a long journey. "Being wearied by His journey," Jesus sat by a well. Jn. 4:6. A woman of Samaria approached to draw water.

Jesus is thirsty. But when Jesus saw the woman, He saw a much greater need. He saw a woman that was thirsty spiritually - a woman who was parched and dehydrated. She had a huge well inside of her that was completely dry.

Not only was the woman empty inside, she was lonely and emotionally isolated. She was wandering in a relational desert - desperate to fill the void within. She had been through five different husbands, and now lived with a man to whom she was not even married. Jn. 4:18. Her need was great.

Jesus is thirsty. As the woman approaches, Jesus makes a request, "Give Me a drink." Jn. 4:7. But strangely, as the story continues, Jesus does not receive a drink. Jesus is thirsty, but He denied His own need. His request is made not for His own need, but the greater need of the Samaritan woman.

First, Jesus' request establishes an immediate connection with the woman. She is not only a Samaritan and a woman. She is also a fallen woman. Jews had no dealings with Samaritans (Jn. 4:9), and until now, the Samaritan woman had only experienced scorn from Jews. But with four simple words ("Give Me a drink"), Jesus cut through centuries of prejudice and hate. To the woman's surprise, Jesus' words conveyed no derision or reproach. "How is it that You, being a Jew, ask me for a drink since I am a Samaritan woman?" Jn. 4:9. Jesus connected with the woman immediately.

Second, Jesus' request focused on the area of her need. Jesus discerned the destitution within, so He directed the Samaritan woman to the source - the key to her salvation. She needed living water. "If you knew the gift of God, and who it is who says to you, 'Give me a drink,' you would have asked Him, and He would have given you living water." Jn. 4:10.

Living water - water that dispels any thirst. Living water - water that becomes in her a "well of water springing up to eternal life." Jn. 4:14. Living water - water that from her innermost being flows as a river. Jn. 7:38. Jesus knew that this Water - the fullness of the Holy Spirit - would fill every longing within her empty heart.

Jesus knew that spiritual water was essential for spiritual life.

This water is necessary for worship - for communion with God. Without it, true worship is not possible. Jn. 4:24.

At that moment, the dry well within the Samaritan woman became a gushing stream of life. She was filled with living water, and she would never thirst again. In her joy, she left her water pot behind, and rushed to the city to tell others Whom she had found.

JESUS IS HUNGRY

Jesus is hungry. He and His disciples have been on a long journey. The disciples go into the city to purchase food. Jn. 4:8. Jesus has taken the time to share with the Samaritan woman, and He has still not eaten. But now townspeople, with whom the Samaritan woman has shared, approach from the city. Jn. 4:30.

Jesus is hungry. The disciples have food and urge Jesus to eat. "Rabbi, eat." Jn. 4:31. But when Jesus sees the townspeople, He sees a much greater need. He sees people that are hungry and thirsty spiritually - people that have a need for the Lord.

Jesus is hungry. As the people approach, Jesus does not take the food that His disciples offer. Jesus is hungry, but He denied His own need. He knew of more needful nourishment. "My food is to do the will of Him who sent Me and to accomplish His work." Jn. 4:34.

What did Jesus mean by this statement? Food is necessary to live. It is essential for our inner being. Jesus is telling the disciples what is necessary for Him spiritually. For Jesus to survive spiritually, He had to do God's will and accomplish His work. If Jesus did not do this work, He would starve spiritually.

PRINCIPLE: Participating in God's work is necessary for us to survive spiritually.

SPIRITUAL FOOD

What is this spiritual food? Jesus immediately begins talking about the harvest and the need for His disciples to work in it. Jn. 4:35-38. As Jesus was teaching His disciples about spiritual food, He directs them to a harvest of souls from the city approaching Him at that moment. "Behold, I say to you, lift up your eyes, and look on the fields, that they are white for harvest." Jn. 4:35.

When I became a parent, I thought that I was the teacher, and my children were the learners. I thought I was grown, and my children were growing. I thought that I was the

giver, and my children were the recipients. I was wrong.

One day it dawned upon me that I learned as much from being a parent as my children learned. I realized that I grew as much from being a parent as my children grew. I benefitted as much from being a parent as my children benefitted from being my child.

It is the same in the Kingdom of God. I can not express the impact of my work on me. So many times, as I have returned from an outreach event, I have felt deeply encouraged and uplifted. The ministry feeds upon itself. One activity prompts and enhances the next.

Ministry - real ministry - not only causes me to survive. It causes me to thrive.

Jesus knew of the parallels between our physical body and our spiritual being. Our bodies require water to survive. Without a well of the Spirit dwelling inside of us, our spiritual beings wither and die. It is our spiritual DNA.

Our natural bodies require food to nourish and sustain us. Likewise, our spiritual being requires nourishment from the work of God. If we do not participate in the work of God in the harvest, we languish and die spiritually. This work not only sustains us; it causes us to thrive. Jesus instructed His disciples to look at the harvest, and to enter into it.

LABOR OF LOVE

When Jesus teaches the disciples about the work of God that nourishes, He speaks of labor in the harvest. Jn. 4:38. Make no mistake, the labor in the field is hard work. Bringing disciples into the Kingdom of God is hard work. It takes time and effort. It takes self sacrifice and sleepless nights. It takes patience and diligence.

We want to sit and let God do it all. But Jesus makes it clear that He is deputizing us to do the work of the Kingdom. "Those who diligently seek Me will find Me." Pro. 8:17. When we "seek" God, we often want God to come to us. Sometimes, though, He wants us to search for Him. We need to go and find where He is working. When we align ourselves with His work, then we experience Him in that work! We need to go into the fields for our own nourishment. That is His will and command.

Work is another hallmark of spiritual DNA. Humans are motivated by their work. We find pleasure and satisfaction in the business process. A job well done is fulfilling, and it spurs us to continue our efforts.

I have represented one businessman, Wright, for many years. Wright specializes in "turnarounds." A "turnaround" takes a failing business, salvages its viable aspects or divisions, and turns the business into a profitable and thriving company.

Wright has functioned at high corporate levels. He has taken over dying manufacturers and retailers, and made them into multi-million dollar companies. Not all of his endeavors are success stories. The risks are great. If the turnarounds work, they pay off handsomely. If they fail, the companies and the investors lose everything.

Wright has made millions of dollars in his life. But he hasn't hoarded the money. For a long period, it seemed that Wright went from success to failure to success to failure. Each time he made a huge bundle on a turnaround, he put the whole bundle into the next venture, often losing it all. But Wright never seemed to be flustered by failure. He kept resurrecting his enterprise with the next project.

One day, I asked Wright, "Why don't you keep some of the money for yourself? You would be a multi-millionaire!"

Wright winked at me and said, "David, it isn't the money! It's the thrill of the chase!"

Wright is now 75 years old, and working hard in his next turnaround.

For many persons, work is not just about earning money. It is the process itself that charms them. Success from their labor is joyful, but they also delight in laboring for that success.

Jesus gave a clear instruction – "Do not work for the food which perishes, but for the food which endures to eternal life." Jn. 6:27. If we have spiritual DNA, we love to work in the kingdom. We experience great joy in the harvest; but the work itself nourishes and sustains us.

PRINCIPLE: The nourishment of work arises from both the result and the process.

BEING AND DOING

Understand what happened to the Samaritan woman. Jesus taught her about living water. Out of her experience, she instinctively began doing God's work. The harvest of souls that approached Jesus as He taught the disciples about spiritual food was a result of her work. From her being flowed the doing. They are intertwined. True spiritual drink led to true spiritual food.

In John 15, Jesus tells His disciples to "abide in Me." Jn. 15:4. This abiding is our spiritual drink. But Jesus continues, "He who abides in Me, and I in him, he bears much fruit." Jn. 15:5. This bearing fruit is our spiritual food. When you submit to God, and participate in His work, you are engaged with Him. Being who we are in Him leads to doing His work.

"By this is My Father glorified, that you bear much fruit, and so prove to be My disciples." Jn. 15:8.

If there is an emptiness within, consider your spiritual need - a need for spiritual water and a need for spiritual food. Consider how Jesus quenched His thirst and satisfied His hunger.

Thereafter, Jesus stayed with the Samaritans and the Samaritan woman for two days. Those were two days of complete peace; deep fulfillment; enriched faith; and joyous pleasure.

MEDITATION: "Those who sow in tears shall reap with joyful shouting.

He who goes to and fro weeping, carrying his bag of seed,

Shall indeed come again with a shout of joy, bringing his sheaves with him." Ps. 126:5-6.

1. Have you experienced the joy of the harvest?

2. Have you sown in such a way that you expect a harvest?

3. What specific steps can you take to improve your spiritual health?

REVIEW:

1. Rivers of Living Water quench spiritual thirst.

2. Work in the harvest field is spiritual food.

3. Labor in the Kingdom fuels the disciple.

4. Our being in Him leads to our doing His work. They are inseparable.

POSTLOGUE

"I don't have the ability to go out and make disciples. It scares me."

"I can't do everything it takes to model and teach and train and release. What should I do?"

"Do I really have to disciple small groups of people from beginning to end?"

I hear concerns like these statements from church members all the time. My initial response is "You are right. You do not have the ability to make disciples. Neither do I. But Jesus does have this ability, and He abides in you and in me. And His instructions are unmistakable." Paul is a man who made many disciples. Hear the faith of this statement from Paul. "I can do all things through Him who strengthens me." Phil. 4:13.

It is difficult for many church members to make disciples. Most churches are established on the strong ministry (often a strong pulpit ministry) of one leader. That dynamic meets the expectations of the leader, because the church members (often in large numbers) come to hear that leader "minister." The church members are trained to sit and listen.

It is possible to lecture in large numbers. It is, however, virtually impossible to train for ministry in large numbers. As a result, many Christians are well taught, but are poorly trained. They know how to sit and listen, but not how to fulfill the ministry of Jesus. Chances for revival will greatly increase when Christian leaders train in small numbers as eagerly as they lecture in large numbers.

The correct response to *"What should I do?"* is: Do what God has called you to do. He has a ministry for each person, and He calls each of His followers to specific ministry. That ministry may be to disciple small groups of people from beginning to end. That ministry may be to work in one small, specialized part of discipleship - such as evangelism, growth, teaching, training or release. God alone has the answer. God has made each person uniquely so that person can fulfill a particular role in His Kingdom. He has a plan for your life. We will explore keys to finding that plan in the next book. Your part is to seek, understand and obey God's will for your life. By doing so, you will fulfill the ministry of Jesus.

"So then do not be foolish, but understand what the will of the Lord is." Eph. 5:17.

NOTES:

NOTES:

NOTES:

NOTES:

NOTES:

www.ingramcontent.com/pod-product-compliance
Lightning Source LLC
Chambersburg PA
CBHW081258040426

42452CB00014B/2554